BOAT ARMAMENT

OF THE

U. S. NAVY.

DESIGNED BY AND EXECUTED UNDER THE DIRECTION OF

J. A. DAHLGREN,

COMMANDER U. S. N.

IN CHARGE OF THE ORDNANCE DEPARTMENT U. S. NAVY YARD,

WASHINGTON, D. C.

SECOND EDITION.

PHILADELPHIA:

PRINTED BY KING & BAIRD, 9 SANSOM ST.

1856.

TO

MY ESTEEMED FRIEND

AND

FORMER COMMANDER,

COMMODORE JOSEPH SMITH, U. S. N.,

CHIEF OF BUREAU OF YARDS AND DOCKS,

THESE PAGES

ARE MOST RESPECTFULLY

INSCRIBED.

CONTENTS.

BOAT ARMAMENT.

"L'efficacité de l'artillerie est entièrement subordonnée à l'intelligence et à l'addresse du cannonier et à la capacité de l'officier qui le dirige."

THIROUX.

INTRODUCTORY REMARKS.

It is now four years since the Memorandum was printed by order of the Bureau of Ordnance, for the use of the officers of the Navy, in order to explain the System of Boat Armament then recently adopted.

The number printed has been nearly exhausted, and other occupation has alone prevented me from preparing a second edition, some time since, with such corrections and additions as the tests of service or farther investigation should have rendered proper.

It is gratifying to me that, on the whole, the plan and its details have proved efficient, and have encountered fewer difficulties than usually attend the first practical initiation of a new project. And that its general utility has been recognized in several instances, where light artillery has been needed in boats or in landing detachments of seamen.

When the war with Mexico commenced, the Navy of the United States suddenly found itself called upon to act in a sphere almost foreign to its previous experience, and not only the least suitable to its means, but certainly the least to be preferred of all others in which a Navy can be employed.

The peaceful tenor of the national policy since the war of Independence, and our territorial isolation from the great nations of the world, had induced little occasion or necessity for collision with any of them; and when this had occurred, the wide Ocean that lay between the shores of these States and our antagonists for the time, naturally made that Ocean the field where our small Navy resorted for action. This, with its limited force, and the impracticability of operating with any effect upon the territory of the enemy, served to confine our vessels to the legitimate and more agreeable task of a naval force,—ship met ship, and heavy cannon wielded with skill by some ot the ablest seamen of that or any other day, decided the victory. Thus it was in the offensive operations against Revolutionary France, in 1798, and against England, in 1812; and hence the entire attention of our young Navy was, happily for its early vigor, engrossed by the first and highest purposes of its creation, and diverted from subordinate ends which could afford but scanty laurels.

But when the war with Mexico began, that power being destitute of a sea-force, our Navy had no alternative but to proceed by the usual mode of blockade and coast warfare; for which it was so little prepared, that the means were necessarily to be improvised. Our lightest Sloops of War had too much draft to venture in the shoal water that bordered the hostile shores, or to pass the sand-bars that blocked the channel-ways of the rivers,—while the absence of even a semblance of an armament for Boats was too apparent. A few old iron carronades and some specimens of the antique mortar-howitzer were to be seen about the yards, and occasionally they found their way afloat. But not a shell was provided for them, and shrapnel were unknown to the service as a part of the equipment.

The Navy was not slow in finding a remedy. Light vessels, purchased from the coasting trade, were armed as well as possible, and everything that was at hand in the way of light artillery was put in requisition for the Boats. Field 6 pdrs., 12 pdrs., and mountain-howitzers from the land service, with the iron carronades, and a few old $4\frac{2}{5}$ inch howitzers that were hunted up in the storehouses of the yards, furnished something to begin with,—and however heterogeneous the medley, it is due to all concerned to say that the immediate purpose was well met. The Mexican coasts, Atlantic and Pacific, were so completely lined with cruisers, that no privateer could issue thence to annoy our commerce, whose canvass whitened every sea. Our sailors were found, at Tabasco and Tampico, co-operating ashore in the general cause as well as the case admitted. And on the Pacific coast, the conquest of a large territory by the Naval forces stood by itself unrivalled, the only instance of the kind, and more than compensated for the absence of other opportunities of distinction.

There was an imperative necessity, however, for providing more fully against the recurrence of such an emergency; and having then quite recently found myself in charge of the Ordnance duty, at the Washington Navy Yard, I presented to Commodore Warrington, Chief of the Bureau of Ordnance, a proposition for creating a suitable system of Armament for Boats. This was received favorably by that distinguished veteran, and with rather scanty means, I proceeded from one step to another, until the present system was completed.

The disadvantages of limited resources and experience were, however, fully compensated by the untrammelled use of those resources, and the hearty support I received from the Chief of the Bureau of Ordnance. If there were no reliable antecedents to follow, neither were there any of an opposite character to avoid. The field was open for full investigation.

The initial step was made in the autumn of 1848, with a little piece somewhat larger than a mountain-howitzer. But it was not until June, 1849, that I was able to furnish the first piece for service to the U. S. Ship John Adams, then fitting under Captain Powell, for the coast of Africa.

Since that, the means at my disposal have increased. A regularly organized Department has grown up from the germ of 1848, and a fine building* affords ample space for the increased quantity of machinery, with the steam power that drives it, and separate rooms for the fitting of shell, shrapnel, &c. I have also but recently completed and put into operation a foundry for bronze howitzers, in which several pieces have already been cast, and the results removed all doubts as to the successful operation of the furnace, which works well: it is capable of containing ten thousand pounds of metal in fusion.

The foundry is at one end of the principal building,—the laboratory at the other, forming three sides of a square; and the entire process from the raw material to the complete arm in action may be witnessed in passing from one division to another of the establishment. The casting of the howitzer—the quality of its metal as shown by the combination of the constituents,—the tensile strength per square inch, specific gravity, &c.—the boring, turning, and finishing of the howitzer,—the construction of the carriages for the boat and the field,—

* Two hundred and fifty feet in length, completed and occupied in May, 1854.

the casting of the projectiles, their inspection, manufacture of the fuzes, the fitting of the canister, shrapnel, and shells; the drilling of the Ordnance seamen,—and lastly, the practice with shrapnel, &c., from the howitzer in the launch on the river, or on its field carriage ashore.

A considerable number of boat-howitzers have been issued for service; some have even been mounted in vessels intended for distant surveying service, where the proper batteries were not needed, and the space they occupied was wanted for other purposes. The Vincennes, Steamer Hancock, Porpoise, Kennedy, Steamer Water-Witch, had each a 24-pdr. howitzer pivoted on the forecastle, and two 12-pdr. howitzers (750 lbs.) on the quarter-deck.

These, however, were only designed to make signals, and to alarm the savages who might be troublesome in the course of the work, not as suitable for offensive purposes in which even vessels of this class might be engaged.

I shall not attempt to institute any comparison between the system of boat-armament designed by myself, and what had preceded it.

The latter is duly represented in this department by a number of its best pieces, which I have collected from different quarters of the general service, and it may be said emphatically that they have great historic interest, of no recent date either—as there are among them, two or three of the old $4\frac{2}{5}$ inch mortar-howitzers used as far back as the Tripolitan war.

One little piece, in particular, is noteworthy, being that which was used so injuriously against the seamen of the U. S. Frigate Savannah, who, during the war with Mexico, were landed to relieve an interior post in California, then in some danger. Its weight is about 156 lbs. and that of the ball $2\frac{1}{2}$ lbs.

It is a rough casting, without any exterior finish, swollen at the breech by the action of the charge, and altogether such a petty, miserable looking piece, as to seem utterly contemptible; and yet it figured in several affairs, (for the want of better) was captured with other compeers at the Angels, by Commodore Stockton, and finally found its way to the U. S. Ship Cyane, where it was made to do service against its former owners. To such inferior military means were both parties compelled to resort in contesting the possession of the distant and nearly uninhabited region that now teems with labor and gold.

It may be noted, however, of the system, about to be described—that the weights of its pieces are fully as great as the boats of the navy are capable of carrying,—that the capacity of this weight is developed conformably to the most commonly received opinions upon the subject; and that the power of each piece is quite as great with reference to its peculiar object, as the weight of metal employed admits of—the projectiles being shell, shrapnel, and canister.

The boat-carriage allows the howitzer to be pointed, wherever it can be fired without injury to the crew, the boat preserving its onward course; while with the ordinary carriage, the piece can be trained very little from the direct line ahead, and to fire a-beam or abaft the beam, it is necessary to bring the boat around.

As a consequence, a boat may, with one arrangement, use her powers of speed and offence, or defence, to the full advantage of both; while with the other it is impossible, and one must be sacrificed more or less to the other.

The field-carriage is but half the weight of that used in the army for corresponding pieces. It is readily stowed in the same boat with its howitzer and the boat-carriage,—can be got out of the boat in debarking whenever such an operation is possible, and is drawn with ease by hand.

The strength and working of the carriages and all the appliances, have been and are still constantly subjected to the tests of practice at this place, by firing on the boat and field-carriages, evolutions on the water and debarking along the shores of the river, to an extent which rarely falls within the opportunities of ships in general service.

The inapplicability of the artillery borrowed from the land service, to naval purposes, was obvious in the Mexican war; and Commodore Perry, who was most actively engaged along the Gulf coast, had occasion at the time to urge this upon the attention of the Bureau. The squadron employed under his command, in the recent expedition to Japan, was supplied with twelve of the present boat-howitzers;

they are said to have been handled with admirable exactness and celerity, and some of them generally attended the debarking parties from the ships. The able commander of the expedition had thus an occasion to contrast the operations of the new boat-howitzers with those of the pieces he had previously been obliged to use in the Mexican war, and it is gratifying to know that he can bear witness to the utility of the change.

It was reasonable to expect that the trying ordeal of service, would disclose many imperfections in a system made up of so many details; but the examination of a number of howitzers and their carriages that have been returned here after long service at sea, afford no reason for departing from the principle or material of construction first adopted, except in the substitution of composition for the iron fastenings of the boat-carriage—for the latter readily rust, which interferes with the use of the carriage, and injures the wood when in contact with it.

In prosecuting the work, it was my good fortune to enjoy the full confidence of the Chief of the Bureau of Ordnance, Commodore Warrington. This gallant veteran is now no more. After faithful and distinguished services, commencing at Tripoli, some half a century since, he was called away in the vigor of mind and body.

No man ever possessed the attributes of a brave and high-minded officer in a greater degree; always clear, prompt and resolute, he was not less successful in administering the Ordnance affairs of the Navy, than as a commander in battle. To the end of his long career, he trod the path of usefulness and honor in the service of his country.

My thanks are due to Captain de Brettes, of the Polytechnic School, Paris, for the trouble he may have experienced in giving the "Memorandum" the translation into his own language, which has recently been published in Paris.

GENERAL ORDER.

The following regulations for furnishing boat guns and field pieces to vessels of the Navy, have been prescribed by the Department.

1st. All boat guns and field pieces, are to be of bronze, of howitzer form, and are to be chambered.

2d. They are to be of 12 pdr. and 24 pdr. calibre; are to weigh not more than 450, and 750 lbs. for the 12 pdrs., and 1200 lbs. for the 24 pdrs.

3d. Ships of the line and frigates, are to have one boat gun of 24 pdr. calibre, and one field piece of 12 pdr. calibre, with a suitable carriage for each.

4th. The guns will be made after plans approved by the Bureau of Ordnance, and prepared with its sanction under the superintendence of Lieut. Dahlgren, upon whose plan all the necessary carriages will be made.

5th. For each 12 pdr. for the above mentioned classes, there shall also be a boat carriage prepared, by which a field piece and a boat gun, or two boat guns, as may be found necessary by the nature of the service, may be used.

6th. Vessels below the class of a frigate, and of not less rate than a second class sloop of war, shall each have a boat gun, which is to be a 12 pdr. mounted complete for boat service.

7th. Hereafter, it may be deemed proper to extend the allowance of boat guns to the smallest class of sloops of war, and field pieces to first class sloops; but that will in a measure depend upon the facility with which they can be prepared, and the service on which they may be expected to be engaged.

WILL. A. GRAHAM,
Secretary of the Navy.

NAVY DEPARTMENT,
December 17, 1850.

CHAPTER I.

HISTORICAL SKETCH OF HOWITZER.

THE purposes to which the Armament of Ship's Boats is likely to be applied, and to which indeed it is restricted, obviously indicate the howitzer as preferable to any other species of light artillery for that service.

In all such cases, it is *personal* and not material which is properly to be the object of fire, and for this, the action of Shell or Shrapnel is far more effective than that of solid shot; the former being divided into numerous fragments, any one of which is capable of sufficient execution; and this extends its power over many objects, while the concentrated effort of the solid shot is superfluously expended upon one or a few objects.

For which reason it is best that, whatever the weight of projectile which can be discharged by any Boat gun, it should have the form of a Shell or Shrapnel; and accordingly this has been done in arranging the system of Boat Armament for our Navy.

The early history of howitzers is involved in much obscurity, and there is little satisfactory information in regard to them previous to the close of the seventeenth century.

About this time ricochet fire was brought into vogue by the distinguished Marshal Vauban,* and bombs as well as shot, were applied to the practice, for which it was customary then to use very low charges; so that the projectile, with no great range to the first graze, rolled along the ground and finally burst. The mortar being unnecessarily heavy for this purpose, a reduction of its weight gave additional facility for transportation with some suitable changes in the mode of mounting; and hence, probably, resulted the howitzer then adopted.

Pieces of this description constituted part of the field train of the Dutch in 1693, when they, with the English and other troops, defended a position between Nerwinden and

* Proposed in 1688, and executed successfully at the siege of Ath, in 1697.

PLATE 1

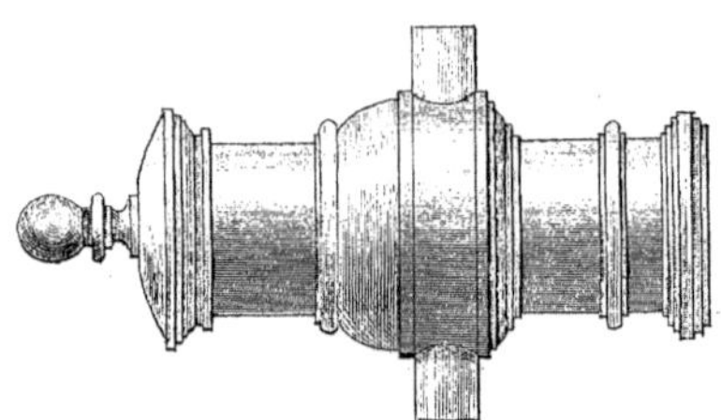

ENGLISH HOWITZER

NERWINDEN 1693.

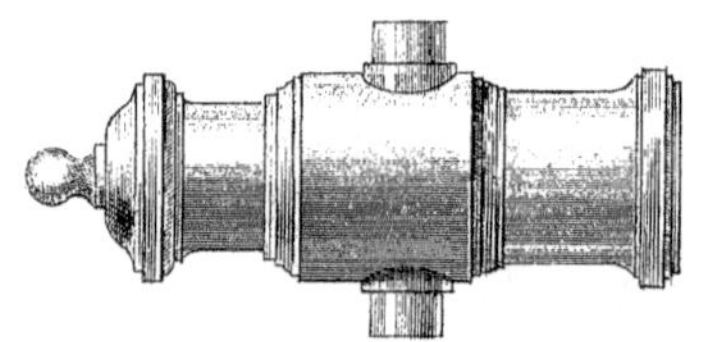

REVOLUTIONARY TROPHY

YORKTOWN 1781

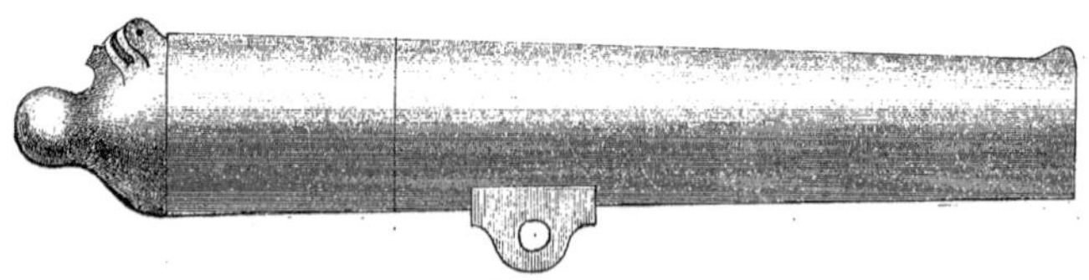

U. S. BOAT HOWITZERS 24 PDR.

(BY J. A. DAHLGREN.)

1849.

D. Chillas Lith. 80 S. 3. St. Phil.

another village, covered by a hasty entrenchment, under the immediate command of King William; they were driven from it by the French after some hard fighting, and eight of their howitzers captured, two English and six Dutch.*

During the 18th century, the piece seems to have been unchanged in form or in the mode of its application, excepting in the artillery of one power.

In the annexed sketch are represented two howitzers:—

The first is an English howitzer, taken at Nerwinden, in 1693.

The second represents a French howitzer, cast in 1778, at Douay, by Berenger; it fell into the hands of the English, and was surrendered by them at Yorktown, the scene of the closing struggle of the war of Independence. It is now preserved at the Washington Navy Yard.

It does not appear that the French artillerists felt or admitted the necessity of the new piece very readily,† as it was not mentioned among their ordnance as late as 1734, in a

* Saint Remy, ii. 30.

† Thiroux.

royal decree, which fixed the dimensions of "*Canons, Mortiers, et Pierriers.*" At the battle of Fontenoi (1745), there were none in the French field train,* and according to military writers,† it was not until 1749 that some 8-inch howitzers were cast by La Vallière.

It was reserved for Frederick of Prussia to assign the howitzer a part suitable to its power. He is said to have assembled forty-five of these pieces at one position during the battle of Burkendorf (1762.) Among the many felicitous conceptions and improvements in artillery of the warlike monarch, none perhaps exerted more influence than this; the howitzer, which previously had met with little favor, at once emerged from obscurity, and ever since has constituted an important part of every field train.

The lessons given by this warrior were not neglected by the recipients. In France nothing short of an entire re-organization followed, and for this purpose General Gribeauval was recalled and entrusted with the task. In his system, as in the Prussian, the pieces for

---

* Paixhans, Thiroux. † Thiroux, M. Meyer, Durtubie.

field service were entirely separated from the siege train, and made much lighter; a 6-inch howitzer was also introduced specially for the field service (1765.) This piece was a decided improvement on the 8-inch howitzer, but still, though the step was in the right direction, it was evident that the original idea was not departed from to any material extent.

Nor does it seem from the writers of the day that such was contemplated. General Durtubie* says:—

"The howitzer is a kind of mortar, a little longer than common, and is mounted on a field carriage."

In the wars of the French Revolution and Consulate, the services of the howitzers caused them to be regarded with much favor—but when opposed to the superior efficiency of the Prussian howitzers, or contrasted with the direct and powerful fire of the field-guns, with which they were associated, the common opinion seemed to demand such changes as would enable the shell and its piece to perform the part they were believed to be capable of.

---

* Manuel d'Artilleur, 1795.

This is expressed in a communication on the subject, addressed by the Committee of Artillery to the Minister of War, in 1800:—

"Ici il n'est pas question de changer, il faut créer."

Which denotes very clearly a conviction that the howitzer of that day, and its method of execution, should give way to something more efficient; and accordingly, the next step shows that ricochet fire was to be merely incidental to the chief purpose, and that the howitzer was no longer to perform a subordinate but a leading part.

In 1803, the 24-pdr. howitzer was added to the French field batteries, and like the 6-inch howitzer, was associated with the 8-pdr. cannon. The weights of these howitzers being nearly alike, and the differences in other respects as follows:—

	6-inch.	24-pdr.
Diameter of bore . .	6,53 in.	6.00 in.
Length of bore . .	4.14 cal.	5.00 cal.
Weight of shell . .	25 lbs.	$16\frac{3}{8}$ lbs
Weight of charge . .	17 oz.	
Weight of piece . .	723 lbs.	648 lbs

The tests of practice, however, and these were soon obtained in the Wars of the Empire, made manifest that, though the new piece was in advance of the old howitzers, yet, like them, it was inaccurate, so violent in reaction as to damage its carriage, and still very inferior in power to those of other nations. The Emperor, therefore, added the captured Prussian and Spanish howitzers to the *material* of his artillery*.

This gradual advance in the French service had been preceded by the Russian artillerists, who, after the Seven Years' war, adopted the long and heavy howitzers, termed licorns.† The power of these more than matched that of the French howitzer, as well as the Prussian and Spanish, and Napoleon had directed experiments to be made with them, looking to some farther changes, when his misfortunes intervened.

In 1813, the French artillery consisted of 27,936 pieces;‡ at the peace of 1815, the howitzers included in this immense quantity

---

* Paixhans. † M. Meyer. ‡ Instr. d'Artillerie.

of artillery were of the following various descriptions:

The 8-inch howitzer, } Gribeauval.
The 6-inch howitzer, }
The 24-pdr. field howitzer of 1803.
The Prussian heavy 6-inch howitzer.
The Spanish field howitzer of 6-in.

Of these it is remarked by an able writer: —"The first three were inaccurate, had little range, and were so violent in reaction as to destroy their carriages, even when strengthened. The 4th and 5th are better; but the Prussian was too heavy for the batteries of divisions. The Spanish 6-in. not so powerful for reserve as its class should be."—(*Paixhans.*)

The Committee of Artillery continued their labors, and one of the results has been the adoption of two howitzers, for the field train, of the longest and heaviest description, the 15-cent. and 16-cent.

The total change now wrought in the character of the piece will be perceived by contrasting the two which use shells of like weight, viz.: The 6-in. of Gribeauval with the new 16-cent. howitzer.

		6-inch.	16-Cent,
Bore,	Length,	4.14 cal.	10.78 cal.
	Diameter,	6.53 in	6.52 in.
Weight,	Projectile (loaded,)	25 lbs.	25 lbs.
	Charge,	17 oz. ($\frac{1}{23}$)	$3\frac{1}{3}$ lbs. ($\frac{1}{8}$)
	Piece,	723 lbs.	1950 lbs.
Initial velocity,		800 feet.	1200 feet.

The charge of the new piece is three times greater than that of the 6-in., and the initial velocity of its shell one-half greater.

Thus it will be seen that the result of severe experience had made plain the necessity of giving greater velocity to the howitzer-shell, and the French system had gradually, in the course of more than half a century, advanced from the light 8-in. and 6-in. to the long heavy 15-cent. and 16-cent.

Of the five principal European powers, three followed the more recent views, viz.: England, France, and Russia; while two adhered to the primitive idea, viz.: Austria and Prussia.*

"En Allemagne on a généralement conservé l'obusier court, dont on envisage l'emploi en campagne sous un autre rapport que nous le faisons en France; Les Allemands sont donc restés fidèles à l'idée première de l'obusier que ne parait avoir guère été, à l'origine, qu'un mortier placé sur un affût à roues." (Favé.)

CHAPTER II.

WEIGHT, CALIBRE, AND CONSTRUCTION OF THE UNITED STATES BOAT HOWITZERS.

The classes of howitzers necessarily vary, the weights being determined by the capacity of the boat at the bow and stern, where it is the invariable practice to carry and use light artillery.

The launch, being the largest and strongest of the ship's boats, is, therefore, appropriated to the carrying of the heaviest of the light artillery, as well as to many other services in which size and strength are most needed. None of these purposes is more important than that now in view, as it measures the offensive power of a ship beyond the reach of her heavy ordnance. It is therefore of consequence that, in designing launches, this object should be strictly borne in mind.

Fine lines may conduce to appearance or to greater speed, but they lessen the buoyancy forward and circumscribe the space within the gunwale—Hence, the piece proper to the size of the launch, cannot be borne or handled efficiently, and a very material advantage is abandoned unnecessarily.

A launch should always have sufficient fullness at the water-line of the bows, so as to afford the buoyancy required to sustain its appropriate gun, and such a form of gunwale as will permit the muzzle of the piece to look well over it around the entire sweep, thus avoiding the liability of having the bow shattered or set on fire by the explosion.

For the same reason, the ordinary projection of the stem above the gunwale is to be entirely suppressed, and the sheer of the lines forward also, using the temporary washboard, if needed, to keep dry in a sea-way.

In cutters, the stem and the sheer may also be made to conform to the convenience of the guns which they are to carry, and the heaviest of such boats should have the bow to approach in fullness that of the launch, rather than the acuteness of the smaller and swifter cutters.

Faults of the kind above mentioned, are noticeable in the launches of some of our recently constructed ships, which are, in this way, liable to a material diminution of power where expeditions are concerned, because they are unable to carry a proper gun, or else to use it efficiently.

It is well ascertained that the launches of frigates and the heavier ships, are fully capable of carrying forward or aft, pieces as heavy as will be required for any service to which the boats are likely to be applied.

The launch of a line-of-battle ship, for instance, would bear, without difficulty, a piece of 2000 lbs., which amount of metal would construct a 32-pdr. howitzer. But as this class of ships is rarely commissioned in our navy, and a piece so heavy would be too burdensome for the boats of any other ship, it seemed injudicious to divert the operations of a new and limited establishment from the fabrication of pieces required daily to supply the current demands of the classes of vessels most generally used.

A 24-pdr. howitzer, of about 1300 lbs., was therefore adopted for the heaviest class as more suitable to the immediate and pressing wants of the Navy, as it could be carried by a frigate's launch, if any occasion should require the exhibition of much force in boat expeditions, while it would be no insignificant piece for the launch of a 74, when the necessities of service should cause a ship of that class to be commissioned.

The howitzer, specially designed for the frigate's launch, is the 12-pdr. of 750 lbs.; a piece which, in all probability, combines efficiency and mobility in a higher degree for boat operations than any other, and there is little doubt that the experience of active service will confirm this opinion of its merits.

The launch of a sloop-of-war could hardly be expected to sustain the 12-pdr. of 750 lbs. with any convenience. Hence the necessity of a lighter piece that would suit the launches of the least of that class of ships, there being no less than three rates of them. For this purpose, the 12-pdr. howitzer of 430 lbs. is intended.

Hence results the following arrangement:

	Launches.	Cutters.	
24-pr. howitzer,	74's,	——	——
Medium 12-pdr. howitzer,	Frigate's,	74's, 1st.	——
Light 12-pdr. howitzer,	Sloop-of-war's,	Frigate's 1st.	74's 2d.

FORM, ETC.

THE several classes of United States' boat howitzers differ only in weight and dimensions; they are alike in the principle of construction, the arrangements for mounting, manœuvring, and firing.

In their design I have followed the utmost simplicity of figure and dispensed with all external ornament.

Around the charge, the bronze is distributed in the form of a cylinder, extending sufficiently in front of the seat of the projectile; thence to the muzzle it is continued as a truncated cone. The breech-plate is a portion of a sphere, as shown in the sketch.

The bore is terminated by a conical chamber; several reasons might be urged for preferring it to the cylindric; but, so far as concerns these howitzers, the chief inducement was the greater facility for rapid loading, without incurring the least chance of the charge being detained when sent home by the rammer; an expectation which, it is needless to say, considerable practice has fully realized.

The howitzer is mounted by a loop similar to that of a carronade.

PRINCIPAL DIMENSIONS.

	24-pdr.	Medium 12-pdr.	Light 12-pdr.
	inches.	inches.	inches.
Diameter of bore, . . .	5.82	4.62	4.62
True windage . . .	.10	.10	.10
Bore { length including chamber	58.20	55.23	44.00
Bore { in diameters . .	10	12	9½
Chamber, length . . .	6.00	5.23	5.23
Length from B. R. to muzzle-face	58.20	56.23	45.24
Diameter of cylinder . .	11.42	9.00	8.00
Diameter of chase . .	8.82	7.24	6.42
Length of cylinder . .	15.00	12.00	10.00
Length of chase . . .	43.20	44.23	35.24
From base ring to axis of loop	23.75	24.60	18.78
Hole in loop, length . .	7.00	5.00	3.60
do. diameter . .	2.50	2.03	1.50
Weight	1310 lbs.	760 lbs.	430 lbs.

The elevation is performed by a screw passing through the cascabel knob; the ordinary lever for turning it was found entirely inadmissible for convenient and rapid elevation;

and, in lieu thereof, a light disc has been attached just below the thread of the screw. Its edge is coarsely milled, so as to afford a firm touch to the hands.

The lock is a plain hammer perforated at the head, so as to permit free egress to the blast from the vent. It plays in a lug cast on the piece in the rear of the vent, and is so arranged as in no wise to interfere with the pointing of the piece.

A round tangent sight is made to move in a perforation drilled for the purpose, in the rear of the base ring.

In the first howitzers a hole was provided for reeving a breeching, as the arrangements for controlling the recoil had not passed through the ordeal of service. The results of trial here, had to be sure, given reason to believe that they were all sufficient; but by way of precaution, and to meet the possible failure of the design, provision was made for a breeching by a perforation in the cascabel immediately in the rear of the breech plate.

Subsequent service has so fully shown the superfluity of this, that it has been omitted in the recent pieces, much to the advantage of the elevating screw which, by passing through the knob close to the breech plate, is enabled to sustain the action of the howitzer more completely.

If accident should ever disable the compression of the carriage, or the motion in a seaway render it prudent to use a breeching, it need hardly be more than hinted to a sailor that a thimble for the purpose can readily be fitted to the neck of the knob.

PROJECTILES.

The projectiles used in howitzers are shells and canister, to which it is now usual to add shrapnel.

The *canister* is composed of iron shot, weighing 0.16 lbs. each, and 1.07 inches in diameter, packed in a tin case; the interstices being filled with sawdust, the upper end closed with a wrought iron plate, the lower by a wooden block, which is also made to serve as a sabot.

The *shell* and *shrapnel* are cast to gauges differing four-hundredths of an inch from each other; the mean diameter allowing a windage of one-tenth of an inch.

They are made with a hole of one-fourth inch diameter; this is reamed out afterwards so as to receive a wooden plug, into which is placed a fuze, or reamed and tapped for the metallic fuze.

When the founder delivers the shells and shrapnel, they are first inspected and guaged, then put on a lathe in the ordnance-shop and reamed out.

Being transferred to another department of the ordnance, persons selected for the purpose strap them to sabots; if shrapnel, put in the balls, drive in the wooden plug, or screw in the metallic fuze, and attach the charge. All the details of dimensions and weight are regulated with the utmost nicety, and must not only be executed by practised and skilful hands, but, afterwards, be inspected by an experienced person.

When completed, they are stowed in pine boxes, so disposed that the sabot may rest on a ledge in the box, leaving the charge below free from any pressure.

The original arrangements thus contemplated the attachment of the charges to the sabots of the projectiles; but, in the equipment of ships I have been directed to discontinue the practice.

Fixed ammunition certainly has the advantage of great convenience in the hurried preparation that frequently precedes boat operations, particularly at night. Indeed, the impossibility of rectifying any omission in the equipment of boats when they have departed on expeditions, enjoins the absolute necessity of avoiding all possible separation of the several parts of their armament, and an habitual condition for instant employment.

		SHELLS.		SHRAPNEL CASE.	
		12-pdr.	24-pdr.	12-pdr.	24-pdr.
		in.	in.	in.	in.
Diameter*		4.52	5.72	4.52	5.72
Thickness		.70	.90	.45	.55
For wooden plug.	Thickness at fuze-hole†	1.05	1.35	.75	1.10
	Fuze-hole to be reamed to the diameters‡ Exterior	.90	.90	.90	.90
	Fuze-hole to be reamed to the diameters‡ Interior	.743	.698	.788	.735
		lbs.	lbs.	lbs.	lbs.
Weight		8.4	17	6.4	12

AMMUNITION-BOXES, POUCHES, ETC.

The shell, shrapnel, and canister are stowed in boxes of well-seasoned white pine. They are of two sizes. The box contains nine rounds, and the double box eighteen rounds. Each round is accompanied by two primers and one set of fuzes, if the wooden plug is used, in a case of water-proof paper, disposed of in the vacant spaces. The boxes are to be stowed in the stern-sheets, or most convenient place, and, though intended to be water-proof, should, nevertheless, be additionally protected by a tarpaulin.

* Variations allowed to founders—.02 to + .02.

† The interior surface of the reinforce is a plane.

‡ The diameter of the cast hole is .25 in., reamed afterwards as above, the taper being .15 in. to one inch for the common fuze.

A pouch of stout leather, in the form of a passing-box, is issued to each man, in which is to be carried one round of either kind of ammunition. It is slung over the shoulder by a strap, and inside of the cover is a set of fuzes for common shrapnel or shells and two primers, so that any one of the crew is provided with the means of firing one round. In landing, each man has one charge in his pouch, so that, under any circumstances, the piece is supplied with sufficient ammunition for instant action. If the operation is not hurried by the emergency of being opposed at the beach, and the force disembarked is to move to some distance from the landing, one or two double boxes may be lashed under the axle of the field carriage, and each of the gun's crew carry two charged pouches, a weight (25 lbs.) not beyond the capacity of an able-bodied man.* Making, in all, 72 rounds for the howitzer. The pouches are to be replenished from the boxes, and the latter, when emptied, may be thrown aside, if rapidity of movement should become important.

---

* Or the arrangement suggested at page 52 may be resorted to.

CHAPTER III.

BOAT-CARRIAGES.

Each one is composed of three principal pieces.

A—The bed which carries the howitzer.

B—The slide on which the bed moves.

C—And beneath the slide, a wooden plate, connected with the bed by two stout bolts.

The recoil is controlled by compressing the slide between the bed and the lower plate; for which purpose, the bolts connecting the upper and lower pieces have a thread above and a corresponding nut with handles. These are set as firmly as the strength of an ordinary man allows, and will then always suffice to keep the recoil within the limits of the slot in the slide. After discharging the howitzer, the compression is relieved, and the piece run out.

In order that this arrangement may invariably perform its function, it is necessary that the surfaces of the carriage to be in contact should be plane, which will be known to be otherwise when the compression is not found

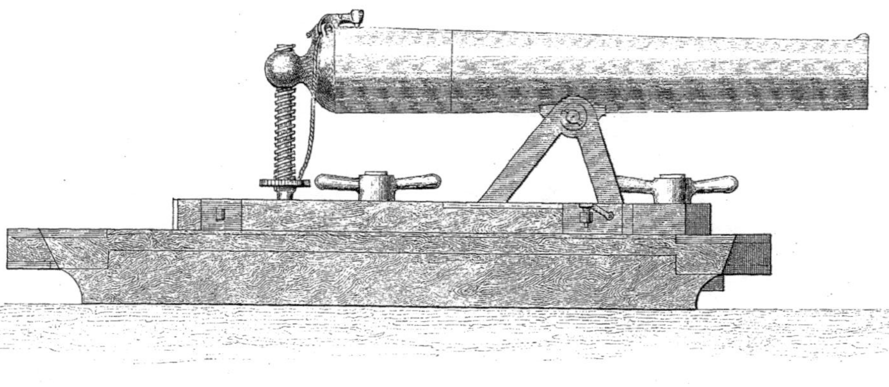

12 PDR. AND BOAT CARRIAGE.

BY J. A. DAHLGREN

D. Chillas Lith. 50. S. 3. St. Phil

to be sufficient to control the recoil. In this case, dismount the gun, take the carriage apart, and examine the surfaces of the three parts. Wherever the coincidence does occur, the wood will be worn smooth; let this be removed in the slightest manner, and the surfaces corrected generally, which will be found to reduce the recoil; but remember that, in making a plane surface, it is by no means necessary to make it smooth; it should be as little so as possible for the present purpose.

If the carriage moves out on the slide with difficulty when the compressors are free, it is owing to the guide in the slot having swelled or warped, and will be easily remedied by removing a very slight shaving from its sides.

With all the care that can possibly be taken in selecting seasoned stuff, it is well known that the continued exposure alternately to sun and rain, incidental to sea service, will for a while warp material of the best quality, and therefore it will be necessary, with a new carriage just sent on shipboard, to examine it occasionally and correct the evil.

The carriages of the heavy howitzers have a piece in front of the bed, holding the forward compressor-bolt. A joint connects the bed with it. This is designed to give the facility of reversing the gun without changing the position of the slide. It is done by taking out a small chock in front of the rear compressor, turning back the connecting straps, releasing the rear compressor, drawing the bed slightly to the rear, so as to clear the attachment, and then pivoting the howitzer round on the rear compressor. The forward compressor is always to be tightened. The operation is readily performed, and the power of checking the recoil undiminished.

Breechings, as already stated, have not yet been used with any of these guns. Should it ever occur that the compression became ineffectual from any cause whatever, a breeching may be rove, and the piece fired as if on an ordinary carronade carriage.

It is not necessary to use tackles to run out the light or medium 12-pdrs., though the weight of the 24-pdr. may possibly require such assistance.

With very little attention, the carriage will be found to perform its part in controlling the recoil even of the most active of these pieces.

The first essay in casting these howitzers here, was a small 12-pdr. weighing 275 lbs., and therefore only equal to thirty-one of its own projectiles. This was mounted on a carriage of the kind now described, and fired with charges of half a pound. The movement allowed by the slot of the slide was 22½ inches, and the average recoil of ten rounds was reduced by the compression to 17 inches.

Increasing the charge to ⅝ lb., and firing four rounds in one minute, the recoils were, 14.01 in., 15.75 in., 19.25 in., and 22.00 in. Average, 17.75 in.

The force of recoil thus resisted may be appreciated by the fact that this piece, being mounted in the bow of a frigate's third cutter, 27½ feet in length, with at least twelve persons in, besides the gun, ammunition, oars, &c., would, when fired, send the boat many yards astern, in smooth water. And yet the application of this force, through the medium of the compression, produced no effect on the frame of the boat—not even the paint over the plank-ends having been disturbed by a hundred rounds, fired chiefly when the boat was under full way.

The carriage of the medium 12-pdr. gave the following results (July, 1849,): Shell, 10 lbs., charge, $1\frac{1}{4}$ ($\frac{1}{8}$); twenty rounds fired; recoils, $16\frac{1}{2}$ in., $17\frac{1}{4}$ in., 16 in., 23 in., &c.; the slot permitted $29\frac{1}{2}$ in. Piece very warm.

The carriage of the light 12-pdr. gave 15 in., 10 in., 12 in., &c. Recoil allowed by carriage, $29\frac{3}{4}$ inches.

The greatest rapidity with which it is desirable to deliver the fire of light pieces, is attainable with this mode of mounting.

A boat-carriage being placed on the experimental battery, the 12-pdr. (of 750 lbs.) which it carried was fired readily at the rate of seven and eight times in a minute, and in a few instances as high as ten times, though it was then found dangerous to the loader, as he could not always get away soon enough from the muzzle of the piece. In this practice, the compressors were always set before firing, relieved afterwards, and the gun pushed out by hand. The limited quarters of a boat, even the largest, afford too little space, however, for such rapid work.

NOTE.—Lieutenant Decamp states that in shelling an African village, near the Cavally river, the howitzer was fired from the launch at the rate of five times in the minute.

CHAPTER IV.

FIELD-CARRIAGES.

The 12-pdr. of 750 lbs. is designed to accompany parties of seamen when disembarked. Its field-carriage is of wrought iron, and considerable difficulty was experienced for some time in reducing its weight to the least limit and yet retaining the strength requisite to endure the recoil. The trail has a small wheel or runner to ease it over any obstacle, and it is found preferable in draught to attach the drag-rope to the trail. The carriage weighs rather less than 500 lbs., and with its piece is drawn readily by the force always disposable from any boat that could carry a gun of this class.

The parts of the carriage are fastened together by screw-nuts. Hence no diffieulty ought to arise in taking it apart, if desirable: the two braces which branch from the trail to the axle have nuts on their ends just outside of the axle; these should have particular attention in course of firing. A pin is driven over them to prevent their being started; but this, too, might be forced out by the severe shock. I have never known it to occur, but, as their security is essential, an eye should be given occasionally to prevent even a possibility of accident.

The axle or pin of the trail-wheel is to be drawn out, and the wheel itself turned up on the trail, in order to moderate the recoil on smooth ground.

This carriage is obviously designed to operate independently of a limber; an addition which would not only increase the countless variety of articles included in the narrow limits of a ship-of-war, but would be very embarrassing if carried in the boat, already lumbered with the gun, its boat-carriage, field-carriage, ammunition, &c.; and, if not, would require a boat for its special accommodation.

If there were an unquestioned necessity for a limber, these difficulties would have to be met in some way; but so far as a judgment may be formed from the requirements of service to which naval light artillery will, in a large majority of cases, be applied, it seems exceedingly doubtful whether there is any reason to justify the addition of a limber to a field-carriage designed exclusively for the ordinary incidents that may attend a cruizing ship.

The chief purposes of naval light artillery may be considered as threefold:—

1. To attack small vessels that are lightly armed, and furnish but slight protection to their crews.

2. To contend with other armed boats.

3. To cover the landing of regular troops.

In either case, the boat-carriage alone is required to manage the gun.

The landing of seamen can hardly be looked on as more than a remote contingency of naval service; one that can seldom occur, and should never be resorted to when opposed by good infantry, or when the object to be attained would take the seamen too far from their boats, which should be the base of operations.

When such an emergency, however, should present, as would warrant the movement of a body of seamen to a distance from the shore, it is supposed that the ammunition slung under the axles, and in the pouches of the men (say seventy rounds per gun,) would fully suffice for any case in which the party should be risked.

When more than a single piece is landed and a march of any distance is anticipated, it will be found convenient to secure the trail of one field-carriage to the axle of another. This can be done by a lashing around the neck of the trail where the thimble for the drag-rope is attached; pieces of stuff or boat's spars are then secured from axle to axle, upon which may be placed the ammunition boxes, provisions, pouches, or other articles carried by the party. Every precaution should, however, be taken to guard against surprise, by keeping parties in advance and on the flanks, as the landing of an armed body of men does of itself indicate a purpose of offence or defense, and suitable preparation for prompt action is therefore absolutely indispensable.

The field-carriage provided, it is believed, will offer greater facility for moving easily than the unlimbered field-carriage of the army, which is in no wise calculated to be so used; and, when limbered up, is indeed a proper draught for horses, while the navy carriage will seldom be found burdensome to a boat's

PLATE 4.

TRANSPORTATION.

Dahlgren's Boat Howitzers

J. Childs Lith.

crew, and at the same time, animal power may be applied, if required.

Referring to the provisions of the French navy for similar cases, it will be seen that the Mountain howitzer (12-pdr. of 220 lbs.) alone is designed for landing, and that its two "caissons," packed over the gun, carry but twelve fixed shells and two canister—a force in metal and supply of ammunition, certainly very inferior to that introduced into our own navy.

CHAPTER V.

AMMUNITION, ETC.

THE shell is the projectile to which the howitzer has always owed its distinctive character. In the old-fashioned short pieces of the last century, these were placed by hand; and no sabots, therefore, required to preserve the fuze in position, as it passed along the bore from the muzzle, in loading.

Grape and canister were also used when the objects happened to be within their range; but shot were excluded from the howitzers entirely, and never furnished to them.

Shells and canister continue to form part of the equipment of howitzers in every service.

Within the last fifty years, another projectile, the shrapnel shell, or spherical case shot, has been contrived, partaking somewhat of the nature of the shell and the canister, and in a great measure superseding the plain shell, where troops are fairly open to its action.

After some discussion, it is admitted by

good authorities, that the conception of this novelty is due, beyond all question, to an English officer, Colonel (since Lieutenant-General) Henry Shrapnel, from whom it now takes its name, with some, while others term it spherical case shot.

Colonel Shrapnel first attempted to realize his conceptions in 1803, at Mount Bay, and seemingly with sufficient success. For, in the operations of the Duke of Wellington in Spain, we find that shrapnel were furnished to the field-guns, and were used, at the very outset, in the battle of Vimiera (1808.)

As might have been expected in the first application of a projectile differing so widely from those to which the artillerymen had been accustomed, the results varied among each other, and produced many discordant opinions. Colonel Napier says, in his account of the siege of Badajoz; "This species of missile, much talked of in the army at the time, was little prized by Lord Wellington, who had early detected its insufficiency, save as a common shell." (Napier, iii. 306.)

At this siege, however, notwithstanding the opinion of the commander-in-chief, shrapnel were used when common shells were just as available, and that under an emergency represented to be of the most urgent nature; so much so, that Lord Wellington determined to risk an enormous loss in his storming columns rather than lose time by following the regular procedure prescribed by the engineer's art.

Under such circumstances, it is fairly inferable that he would insist on the most powerful development of the artillery; and, as his own opinion is stated not to have been favorable to shrapnel, this missile could only have been used because other opinions, to which he deferred, *were* in favor of it.

Subsequently, at the siege of St. Sebastian, the effects were too decided to admit of doubt, and the testimony of the French, who suffered from its effects, is sufficiently convincing.*

In 1811, some cases of the new projectile were captured by the French at the battle of Albuera, and an examination was instituted forthwith; the results of which were rather indifferent; owing, it is said, to the ignorance

---

* "Ce projectile nous fait beaucoup de mal." General Rey to Marshal Soult. (August, 1813.)

of the commission in relation to the true function of the shrapnel.*

The wonderful events that followed, in rapid succession, until the close of the empire, left military men little time or desire for speculations of any kind. Subsequently, it became incumbent on the powers of Europe to reduce the immense establishments which had so long drained their resources: under such circumstances, it was not to be expected that the attention of officers should be seriously bent on professional improvement, when each one felt that he might, at instant notice, be included within the severe reform then in process, and have to seek some other means of livelihood.

A few years rolled by, and the evidences of renovated vigor and means, among the European nations, were noticeable in the cultivation and improvement of their offensive and defensive powers. Among the important objects which then attracted the attention of military men, the shrapnel has occupied a conspicuous place, and to this time it has not

* Fave's preface to Decker, 3.

ceased to stimulate the invention and criticism of all military services: Norway, Sweden, Russia, Austria, Prussia, Saxony, Wurtemberg, Hanover, Denmark, Bavaria, Holland, Belgium, France, Sardinia, and other countries, have contributed more or less to advance the knowledge of the projectile, and to improve its character and application.

As already said, *the shrapnel may be defined to be a combination of the shell and the canister*, by which the former is made to serve as a case or envelop to the balls of the latter. carrying them to the desired point near the object, and then opening to permit their egress. Its sphere of operation can only begin where the dispersion of the common canister becomes too great, and its effect feeble. It certainly does take the place, however, of the common shell to a great extent, where uncovered masses are in view.

It is designed to burst the shrapnel in front of the troops exposed to it, and at just such a distance and height as to disperse the charge of balls among them.

Here the difficulty lies. If the shrapnel bursts too high, too near, or too far, then it is alleged by the objectors that its power is lost, or so far diminished as to be trifling.

The conditions to an execution so exact are said to be :—

1. In appreciating the distance.
2. In timing the explosion.
3. In adjusting its height above the object.

When bodies are moving with velocities of several hundred feet in an instant, spaces of time which it seems ridiculous to attempt the appreciation of by ordinary means, become not only important, but very plain to the perception, by the differences in the explosion.

The importance of knowing the distance can hardly be over-estimated, and the difficulties of making even a tolerable approximation to the truth are not likely to be undervalued by artillerists.

In all circumstances, however, where ordnance is employed, whether in the field or on the water, a knowledge of the distance is the essential element of correct practice in the application of every species of projectile; and the difficulty, therefore, in estimating it constitutes no greater objection to shrapnel than to shell or shot.

Various means have been proposed by military authors for the determination of distances, but in some respect or another they have been deemed faulty, and none of them seem to have met with so much favor as to insure them extensive trial. For it is indispensable that they should not only accomplish the purpose, but also be available within the brief limits permitted by the rapid action and excitement of battle.

The correction of the fire by previous rounds, is a practical means which is instinctively resorted to by artillerymen on all occasions, but is hardly to be relied on in the field within any reasonable extent, when the observer is near the piece fired from; for the angles subtended by the objects, and most especially those of a plane in perspective, are too minute to afford data to the most practised eye. In departing from the line of fire, however, the means of noticing correctly the errors of range increase, and may be of general utility. Boats in line, therefore, can easily amend their elevation of gun and time of fuze, by the signals of those most remote from them.

It is said that, in the field, shrapnel have not the same distinctness of effect as shot. The latter throw up the ground and mark the point of impact very plainly; whereas, the shrapnel explodes in the air, and affords no data for certainly knowing its proximity to the object.

Be this as it may in the field, it is certainly not the case on the water. The jet of water made by every ball is shown clearly at the ranges of greatest useful elevation; and at the point of maximum effect, not many yards in advance of the explosion, the aggregation of these jets makes a line of foam, quickly and distinctly discernible to the operator.

The adjustment of the fuze to the distance, and the altitude of explosion, are regulated to the elevation; and, therefore, the three conditions to good effect may be said to depend mainly on a correct knowledge of the distance.

Considerable experiment will be indispensable to determine accurately the proper relations of elevation of gun, time of fuze, and height of explosion; and systematic practice must be resorted to afterwards in order to familiarize officers to the use, and enable them to make an effective application, of the shrapnel.

It is in the peculiar dissemination of its balls that the shrapnel promises some corrective for errors in estimation of distance. Following the course of the trajectory, with a velocity not less than that of the shrapnel at the instant of explosion, they radiate from the case in the form of a cone; and when projected on the horizontal plane, take an elliptical figure, the greater axis of which coincides with the continuation of the trajectory, and is much elongated, particularly at the low elevations.

There is, no doubt, a point of maximum effect; but, looking to the extent which is covered by this jet of balls, it will readily occur to an observer that, though the maximum effect may be limited almost to a point, yet some departure from this does not reduce the effect considerably, and that a severe execution may take place even if the objects approach the limits of the dispersion.

Almost any practice with shrapnel would illustrate this, if made sufficiently in detail. The following cases, executed here for the

PLATE 5

PRACTICE WITH SHRAPNEL AT SCREENS

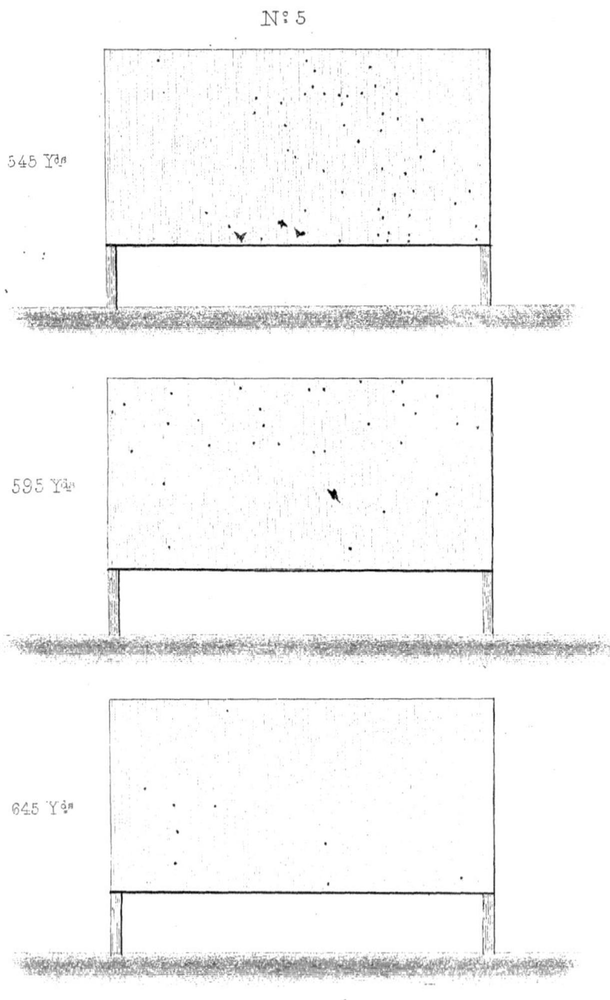

Scale $\frac{1}{120}$

D. Chflas Lith. 50. S. 3. St Phil.

graduation of the sights, will serve for the present purpose.

Three muslin screens were stretched on upright frames over the water, fifty yards apart. In dimensions, they were twenty feet long and ten feet high.

A Frigate's launch, carrying a 12-pounder of 750 lbs. in the bow, was placed 545 yards from the nearest screen.

Its charges were one pound. The elevation by common service sight, as the motion of the boat precluded the use of an instrument for this purpose.

The shrapnel (charged) averaged 11.4 lbs., containing 80 musket balls (17 to the pound,) and four ounces of powder.

The fuzes were two seconds, and such as are issued to the service..

Eight rounds were fired with the following results:—

No. of rounds.	First graze.	BURST.			PERFORATIONS IN SCREENS.			Extreme reach.
		from boat.	in front first screen.	above foot of screen	1st.	2d.	3d.	
	yards.	*yards.*	*yards.*	*feet.*				*yards.*
1	580	No explosion.			1	1	1	
2		474	71	14¾	16	11	4	1767
3		474	71	16	35	11	9	1582
4	524	536	9	2	25	12	2	
5		497	48	18	51	30	7	1747
6		533	12	4¾	1	1	6	1680
7		558	37*	2⅘	1	23	10	1794
8	419	453	92	31¼	13	8	8	1756
		Average - - -			18	12	6	

The gradual increase of the dispersion with the distance is exemplified by the number of balls in each screen, the mean of these eight rounds reducing the effect one-third for 50 yards, and two-thirds for 100 yards.

The results arising then from error in adjusting the explosion, whether from one cause or another, may be inferred from this practice; and, if it should amount to one hundred yards, the object would still be liable to receive several musket-balls.

Still, the explosion should always be made to occur this side of the object, and never beyond it. In the seventh round, the shrapnel

*In front of 2d screen.

passed through the first screen, and burst 13 yards beyond, having only the effect of a shot on it, though it had a good shrapnel effect on the second screen.

The action on ricochet was good, so far as the two instances here given are concerned, and it seems that in the majority of cases the common fuze may be relied on when the ricochet takes place on water; though such practice is not to be recommended with shrapnel.

This amount of firing is entirely too limited to permit any reliable conclusion as to the point where the shrapnel should burst in front of the object, so as to insure the greatest effect; generally, it will be safest to keep it well down on the object when using low elevations.

The Prussian General, Decker, expresses the following opinion (p. 128.) :—

"From the above data, the distances of 60 to 150 paces in front of the object (50 to 129 yards), with heights of four to fifteen feet, have given good results with cannon, apart from the ranges. Information is not yet had in regard to howitzers; and all that we know is, that proper distances vary from 75 to 150 paces (64 to 129 yards,) and the heights from ten to twenty feet apart from the ranges."

The "good results," here mentioned, are what might be called close approximations to the maximum effect; and there is no doubt, as already shown by the data of the same writer, that all the distances in front of the object might be increased, and yet the shrapnel produce considerable effect. Material variation is inadmissible in the height, and very fortunately this is always observable distinctly by the firing party, and can be regulated as may appear best.

The 3d, 4th, and 5th rounds of the practice just given, acting on a boat at the distance of any of the screens, would, in all probability, have disabled nearly every man in it. The 2d and 8th would have exercised a very decisive effect. The 6th at the distance of the 3d screen, the 7th at those of the 2d and 3d. The 1st round would represent the result of a solid shot.

The force of the balls was sufficient, in every instance, to pass through pine boards one inch thick, placed behind the screens, the distance of the third screen from explosion being sometimes 150 yards.

There is a large array of opinion, on both sides of the question, raised in regard to the availability of shrapnel, of which it may be said, perhaps, that while the English authorities have a favorable opinion of the power of the new projectile, their neighbors across the Channel appear to have entertained the opposite view quite as decidedly. Not, however, to such an extent as to preclude examination into the matter; for there is reason to believe that, for several years, the question has been studiously and closely investigated in France, and it will probably form a part of their equipment before long. In a recent publication,* from a quarter that can leave no doubt, of the authenticity of the fact, it is stated: "The shrapnel shell is about to be adopted in France, after the example of several of the European services."

The objections urged repeatedly against shrapnel, and the anticipated frequency of its

---

*Nouveau système d'artillerie de campagne; par L. N. Bonaparte, President de la République.

failure, seem hardly reasonable in view of that admitted to occur in other projectiles commonly used with light artillery, which, with little exception, is immensely disproportionate to the effect produced.

Thiroux,* after citing some cases exemplifying the destruction which sometimes attended the efficient application of artillery, remarks: "But in contrast with such terrible effects, how many shot are thrown away, especially in the attack and defence of places? We could easily quote many cases where long cannonades have ended in no result."

And the commentator† of General Decker says:—"It should not be lost sight of that, in war, there is probably, on an average, not more than one shot in fifty that tells."

In confirmation of these opinions, we are furnished with some facts, by reliable authority, in regard to the number of rounds expended by the French artillery in some of the great battles, alongside of which may be placed the loss, in killed and wounded,

* Instr. d'artill. 73.
† Favé, 312.

assigned by current history to those who sustained this fire.

	Rounds fired by French artillery.	Killed and wounded on opposite side.
Wagram,	80,000	25,000
Leipzig,	200,000	42,600

When it is considered that this carnage was not achieved by the cannon alone, but that the musket, the bayonet, the lance, and the sabre, reaped their full share in the harvest of death, some idea may be formed of the large quantity of shot, shells, and grape that fell harmlessly.

The instances here quoted are two of the severest battles fought by Napoleon, of whom it may be truly said, that he was as incomparable in the use of artillery as of every other arm. At the right time, and at the true point of effort, his matchless genius combined the most immense masses in rapid and precise concentration; and when a crisis arrived, reserves of a hundred pieces were displayed in line with the celerity and force of a thunderbolt.

If, then, the failure of shot and shell be so frequent as represented and generally recognized, it is hardly admissible to slight the shrapnel, until satisfactorily proved to be liable to equal uncertainty: particularly as it is claimed, by advocates of ability and experience, to be less so.

Experiment shows it is far from being infallible, and actual service will no doubt fully disclose its imperfections; but in view of the favorable evidence cited in its behalf by good authorities, it seems more judicious to improve its operation by thorough experiment and practice, and then look to the results for a settlement of the several doubts and issues raised; thus avoiding the equal errors of accepting unreservedly the alleged superiority of this projectile; or of yielding too readily to a scepticism of its real merit without sufficient investigation.

CHAPTER VI.

CONSTITUENTS OF THE SHRAPNEL.

In order that the capacity of the shell which incloses the other components of the shrapnel may be increased to the utmost, its thickness is reduced to the least that will sustain the shock imparted by the charge of the howitzer. Much, therefore, will depend on the quality of the iron, and no effort or expense should be spared to have these shells cast from the best metal, and as uniformly as possible. Such iron as would answer for shot, or even for common shells, would not serve for shrapnel.

Experience, so far, determines the requisite thickness of the shrapnel shell to be about one-tenth of the exterior diameter, which will generally make its weight to be about one-half that of a solid shot of like calibre.*

---

* See page 42.

Besides the spherical form, the oblong has been used in Norway, and the pear-shaped in Wurtemberg.

The charge of powder to burst this case must be the least that will answer the purpose. A few are inclined to think differently, believing that the force of the shell's charge has some influence on the velocity of the balls; but the opinion commonly received is that the office of this charge should be confined to rupturing the case. In the 12 pdr. shrapnel, 4 oz. is used by many services; and it is probable that this is fully sufficient for the purpose; it is the charge used in the shrapnel fitted for the service of the army; and, in the practice with the boat-howitzers, no instance has yet occurred in which it has ignited without bursting the shell.*

Whatever space is left in the cavity of the case by its charge, is to be filled by balls; those of lead are preferable to iron, on account of their greater density, and for other reasons, and are generally used. There is little varia-

---

* With the Bormann fuze and chamber of sulphur, a charge of only one ounce is required.

tion in the size, which is ordinarily that of a musket-ball of 17 to the pound; though trials have been made of balls 14 to the pound, and 22 to the pound.

The shrapnel of our service have 80 ($4\frac{2}{3}$ lbs.) balls in the 12's, and 175 ($10\frac{1}{3}$ lbs.) in the 24's.

The English use $4\frac{1}{2}$ oz. bursting charges, and a less weight of ball.

There is no doubt that balls when loose in the shrapnel are sometimes agglomerated by being fired. This was found to be the case with some that had been suffered to ricochet in sand, the fuze being extinguished. In one, the balls formed a mass, adhering by the edges. Though it never has been noticed that, in bursting, the balls failed to disperse, so that the charge of the shell will probably always suffice to separate them in a great degree when thus adhering together. Occasionally, two have been found firmly united when extracted from the oak timber which was fired at; and a large number of the single balls thus obtained had entirely lost their shape, and were curiously slugged.

It is obvious that, as regards the thickness of the shell, the number of balls, and the quantity of powder contained, there can be no material differences of opinion not easily disposed of by a moderate amount of careful examination. The remaining element, however, the fuze, is likely to furnish abundant matter for discussion, and to require all that consummate skill in theory and practice can effect, in order to arrive at a satisfactory conclusion.

It has already exercised the ingenuity of the officers of almost every service, with various degrees of success: but the attainment has yet been sufficiently short of the certainty desired, to make it clear that much more remains to be done than has been done:*—a conclusion by no means discouraging, if it be borne in mind that military pyrotechny has received little, if any, systematic investigation. So far, indeed, but little of a scientific character has been published on the subject.

One of the essential points in the fuze is CERTAINTY OF IGNITION.

The surface of composition presented to the action of the flame from the charge of the

---

* Decker, p. 51: "La bonne solution est encore à trouver."

gun, is sometimes left smooth and hard, or it is covered with a priming, porous and rough, and in other cases it has a small quick-match worked in, so as to create a greater susceptibilty to the flame. As yet, the practice here indicates no marked differences between the different modes, failures occurring in one about as often as in the other.

Indeed, if we consider the force and intensity of the flame created by the charge of the gun, and the instantaneous encircling by it of the projectile, it would seem reasonable to suppose that any substance of the least degree of inflammability would ignite, if exposed to it in any position.

If so, the smooth hard surface of composition is preferable to any kind of priming, because it is far less liable to deterioration from moisture, which at sea is of the most pervading character, and hardly to be resisted by the softer and porous compositions and matches.

It is not easy to assign any satisfactory reason for the failures that do occur in every species of fuze yet tried. That such is the case no one pretends to deny, and the warmest advocates of any system will say no more than that it will fail in fewer cases than any other.* The failures, however, seldom occur with good fuzes to any extent.

The next requisite for an efficient fuze is REGULARITY IN THE TIME OF BURNING.

This seems yet more difficult of accomplishment than the preceding condition, and it is at least quite as desirable of attainment.

The shrapnel fired from a cannon may have a velocity in the different parts of its trajectory, amounting to as much as 1200 or 1500 feet per second, and hence a difference in the burning of the fuze, almost inappreciable in time, will be made very perceptible by the variations in the distances at which the explosion occurs; thus, with 1200 feet per second, a fourth of a second will produce an error of 100 yards: if the velocity be 600 feet per second, the difference in distance will be still fifty yards.

To one who happens casually to look on

---

* Decker, p. 51: "Car même chez ceux qui croient la posséder il se présente toujours ou des ratés ou des explosions qui se font trop tôt ou trop tard."

when the process of driving fuzes is being executed, it may seem easy to attain the greatest exactness in the results, and indeed hardly possible to avoid it, and Decker asserts it to be within the reach of a commonly intelligent pyrotechnist.* It is, however, impracticable to obtain a column of composition which, *driven and consumed in the direction of its length,* will not give differences in the times of burning equal to considerable fractions of a second, a fact I have been assured of in the course of testing many hundreds of such fuzes.

Referring to the details of shrapnel practice which Decker, himself no mild critic, holds up with evident satisfaction as something of the best, we there note these very variations in the distances of explosion. They do not escape his notice, but he would have them attributable to some unknown action of the atmosphere on the fuze during its flight. It is not easy, however, to conceive the grounds on which this conviction is based, and none are assigned.

The most certain method of producing reg-

---

* Decker, p. 159.

ularity of ignition in the fuze, is, in condensing the loose composition by a single pressure, and causing the ignition to occur transversely to the layer thus formed.

The third important point is the arrangement FOR SECURING THE FUZE, so that it shall not be driven in, or its solidity disturbed by the shock of first displacement.

When the shell is broken in the gun, it may be difficult, sometimes, to distinguish whether this has been owing to the force of the charge or to the premature ignition by the driving in of the fuze.

For although the velocities commonly given in our service to shrapnel, from howitzers, do not exceed 1000 feet per second, it is believed that this arises from a supposed liability of the fuze to be driven in by higher charges. It is the received opinion, however, that shrapnel is most effective with the highest velocities, as these are able to maintain most of their movement, and consequently to impart it to the balls, which are supposed to leave the case with the velocity it has at that instant.

Some of the forms of fuze are very liable to be forced in, and sometimes it is exceedingly difficult to guard them against it. Other fuzes may be considered as nearly beyond the possibility of such accidents; and, therefore, present a very strong claim to consideration on this account alone.

A very common opinion finds a third cause for the breaking of the shrapnel in the ignition of the charge in the shell by the violent friction of the balls during the shock occasioned by first displacement of the shrapnel. But the evidence adduced is quite insufficient to sustain the theory; and a more credible cause of the breaking of the shell will be found in the inferior quality of the metal, or in the displacement of the fuze.

The methods taken in various countries to fulfill the conditions essential to a perfect fuze, differ sometimes in principle, sometimes in detail; and the general interest with which the subject has been pursued, and results exhibited before sovereigns and high functionaries, is very significant of the importance attached to it. A brief notice of some of the fuzes may be useful; premising, however, that, with the best information respecting the official action of the ordnance authorities of a foreign country, it is not possible to speak with exactness thereof; as, in all probability, the most material points are not made known. The requirements of actual warfare alone may be expected to develop the success which has attended the exertions of those who have labored to perfect the shrapnel. When an inventor has given publicity to his method of constructing and using any particular fuze, there are some reliable data for examination.

The feature principally distinguishing one class is, that its composition is disposed in a column, the axis of which coincides with that of the fuze-hole.

To this order belongs the ENGLISH FUZE, the case of which is beech, bored to receive the composition. Three fuzes accompany each shrapnel, cut to the distances of 650, 900, and 1100 yards; and a fourth fuze which is left to be cut as any unusual circumstances may require. In service, the fuze is selected that may be deemed suitable to the distance, or reduced to it by a small drill,* and driven into the fuze-hole at the instant.†

The NORWEGIAN FUZE, by Captain Helwig, resembles the English in the general principle already stated, but differs from it in the mode of construction. The composition is contained in a paper case, which is cut to suit the occasion, and then placed in the wooden tube, which has been previously driven into the shrapnel.

The SPLINGARD‡ FUZE, while it follows the general principle, has also its peculiar method of application. The composition is incased in small copper tubes, about 1.25 inches long, and is received by a wooden tube previously driven into the shell; a cork plug at the top of this sustains the head of the fuze and must exert great influence in preventing the copper tube from being forced in by the first shock.

---

* Fuze-augur.

† Latterly the fuzes of Captain Boxer have been spoken of highly—but we have not sufficient authentic information in regard to them to speak of their merits.

‡ Captain in the Belgian Artillery.

The details are ingenious, and one would be induced to believe that it was very efficient.*

These three will serve to give an idea of several more of the same class, which, with certain modifications, are said to have been used temporarily, or otherwise, in many of the European services.

Of another class, altogether differing in principle and detail, is the ingenious FUZE OF BORMANN, colonel of Belgian artillery.

The discussion which it has produced might, in itself, be cited as no trifling evidence of merit; but we happen to be in possession of far better, the results of actual practice.

Of the good qualities of this fuze no well-founded doubt will be entertained, even by those who, in view of all that can be urged for it, still prefer some other.

Its peculiar principle certainly finds favor in many services, though with some modifications that may have been applied from reason or fancy.

---

* Captain de Brettes speaks in the highest terms of the Splingard fuze—("Etudes sur les fuzés de projectile creux," 42–44.)

In some, the priming magazine on the upper surface has been suppressed, reliance being placed entirely on the small portion of the condensed composition exposed by cutting the plate, thus at once rendering nugatory some plausible objections. In others, the lower magazine has been reduced to a small canal, and this, too, seems to answer the purpose of driving the flame into the shell. And again, some slight changes have been adopted in the form of the outer surface of the plate that covers the composition, so as to facilitate the action of the cutting-tool. In another, an effort has been made to dispense with cutting the fuze altogether, by driving the composition in a detached cylinder made to revolve in a cup; the lower surface of the composition moves over a passage that communicates with the magazine in this cup, and transmits the flame at the time given, by turning the cylinder that has the composition.

All these are mere details, tending, perhaps, to improve the action of the essential principle, but in no wise affecting this first element, nor the claims of its ingenious inventor.

CHAPTER VII.

U. S. NAVAL SHRAPNEL.

THE brief account just given of some of the varieties of fuzes, will suffice to illustrate the difficulties that lie in the way of exploding shrapnel at the exact instant of time required.

Opinion is evidently divided as to the merits of the fuzes that have been contrived by different persons, and practice in actual service can alone show which preference is best founded.

When shrapnel were first introduced into our Navy (1849), as a part of the present system of Boat Armament, the fuzes issued with them were of the kind then used in the Army for such projectiles, and which had gone very creditably through service in the Mexican war.

It consists of a wooden tube, driven into the shrapnel after the balls are put in, which is to receive a paper case containing the composition; five of these are allowed to each shrapnel, their times of burning being respectively 1″, 2″, 3″, 4″, and 5″. They are packed in a paper case, and before the shrapnel is placed in the howitzer, a fuze, of the time supposed to correspond to the distance, is selected and inserted in the wooden tube. The shells of the howitzers were fitted in the same manner.

After the difficulties had been surmounted that lay in the way of the first design and execution of the present Boat Armament, the question in regard to fuzes was reverted to, and scrutinized more closely than before.

In 1851, Major Mordecai, commanding the U. S. Arsenal at this place, and myself, were associated by the War and Navy Departments for the purpose of examining another arrangement of shrapnel; and after ascertaining that it promised some advantage over that in service, we recommended it for partial adoption.

Quite recently, I have been authorized by the Bureau of Ordnance to issue this kind of shrapnel for service in the screw ships now in course of construction.

The following description of this projectile and of the trials to which it and the present shrapnel were subjected in order to ascertain their relative merits, is abstracted from the reports made by Major Mordecai and myself to the Departments of War and Navy, and will serve to indicate the advantages of the new arrangement over that in use.

The case of the common shrapnel is filled with as many musket balls as can be put in loosely, and when the projectile is about to be used, sufficient powder is poured in to fill the interstices. But as the balls, however close they be, have some freedom of motion when the shrapnel is handled or moved, the powder if suffered to remain will be pulverized, and a gradual separation of its constituents will follow, to the prejudice of the force of the charge which, is calculated to be only sufficient to open the shrapnel.

To avoid this, and for other reasons, it is customary to charge the common shrapnel with powder just before being used, and as this must be done previous to the very instant of action, it may follow that more will be prepared than are used; these it is troublesome to discharge afterwards of their contents, for such manipulation of loaded projectiles is never to be recommended on shipboard, and yet, if not done, the shrapnel is liable to the detriment already named.

The commingling of the powder with the balls produces the farther disadvantage of a diffused action, which requires of course a larger charge to open the case, and the disturbing effect which the explosion is supposed to exert on the trajectory of the balls, is thus increased.

In the new plan, the balls are more closely packed, and the interstices filled with sulphur, which solidifies and imbeds the balls, so that they cannot move, and the interior of the shrapnel is filled solidly. A cylindric cavity is also left, the axis of which is coincident with the axis of the shrapnel case, passing through the fuze hole, and extending across the interior. In this is deposited the charge of powder, where it is protected against all injury from the movement of the balls.

By this arrangement the quantity of powder required to open the shrapnel is much lessened, as the new plan requires only $\frac{3}{4}$ths of an ounce, or an ounce, while with the loose balls, four ounces are required. Hence all unnecessary force of explosion is avoided which is supposed to lessen the disturbing effect on the desired course of the balls when the shrapnel explodes in the air as designed.

In this way, also, the probability of premature explosion of the shrapnel, attributed to the attrition of the balls in contact with the powder, is nullified.

The fuze is that already spoken of as invented by Colonel Bormann of the Belgian artillery.

It is a metallic disc, about 1.6 inches in diameter and half an inch thick, made of lead hardened sufficiently for the purpose by the infusion of some tin.*

On the exterior are three turns of a stout thread by which it is to be screwed into the case of the shrapnel or shell. These, as well as the whole form of the metallic disc, are received from the mould in which it is cast.

---

*Colonel Bormann's proportions are :—3 parts of tin and one of lead.—("Exper. sur les shrapnel, par Bormann, Lt. Col. &c.," page 2.)

The composition is firmly condensed into an interior canal of this disc, displayed around its periphery, and as near to it as possible, opening below, and closed after the composition is driven, by a small slip of soft metal pressed in firmly upon the composition.

The upper surface of the disc above the composition is very thin, so as to yield readily to the cutting tool employed to open it. Its whole extent, corresponding of course with the composition below it, is graduated into seconds and fourths of seconds.

The end of the composition where the numeration begins, communicates with a small magazine at the centre of the disc, which is charged with grained powder and slightly closed on the inner side so as to yield in that direction to the explosion.

The operation of the fuze occurs thus:—The thin covering of metal above the composition is cut so as to lay bare the upper surface of the composition, and to afford the flame access to it at the part desired;—the combustion occupies the assigned time in passing from this incision towards the origin of the graduation, when it traverses the orifice leading into the magazine, the contents of which explode smartly towards the interior of the shrapnel case, and there encounters instantly the charge in its chamber of sulphur.

As the metallic disc exposes considerable surface to the shock of movement, it is sustained within by a plate of metal, perforated, to permit the passage of the blast into the shrapnel.

When the case has been properly filled with balls and sulphur, the chamber left in it is filled with powder,—the plate, perforated at the centre, screwed over the orifice,—and the metallic fuze screwed in and well luted around the edge on the exterior surface.

The advantages attributed to the whole arrangement are:—

1st. The composition being condensed by a single pressure of the machine, and the combustion occurring transversely to the stratification of the mass, offers better conditions for uniformity in duration than the common fuze, which is formed of layers compressed successively one above the other, and consumed in the same manner.

2d. The whole error of fabrication, whatever it may be, is only experienced when the fuze is opened at its extreme duration,—at all inferior times it is reduced proportionally, so that an excess or deficiency of two or three tenths of a second at the full extent of the duration, would be limited to $\frac{4}{100}$ths or $\frac{6}{100}$ths of a second if the fuze were cut to one second of time, &c., &c. On the other hand, by using a separate fuze for each time, the whole error of process is incurred in each.

3d. Certainty of ignition and of communicating the flame to the charge of the shrapnel.

4th. Safety against external accident from water and from fire, which is certainly of great importance, particularly when it is considered that boat operations afford but little protection against either.

5th. Security against explosion, in the bore of the piece, which is the most detrimental of all the accidents to which shrapnel or other explosive projectiles are subject; for the round is thus lost, and the bore of the gun more or less disfigured by it.

6th. Greater convenience, because the shrapnel is issued complete and ready for instant use, which is not practicable with the fuzes now used.

PRACTICE WITH SHRAPNEL.

The examination made by Major Mordecai and myself, to test these alleged advantages by firing, was conducted as follows:—

August 7th, 1851.

A 12-pdr., of 750 lbs., mounted in a launch, was anchored in the stream, about 460 yards from a screen 10 feet high and 20 feet long, behind which were two other screens at distances of 50 yards each.

The wind and tide changed the position of the launch during the firing and increased the distance from the screens; which circumstance was of course not favorable to entire exactness in sighting, as the amount of variation in the distance was not known at the time.

The shrapnel were charged with 80 to 84 balls, and $\frac{3}{4}$ to 1 ounce of rifle powder:—

PLATE 8.

SHRAPNEL PRACTICE

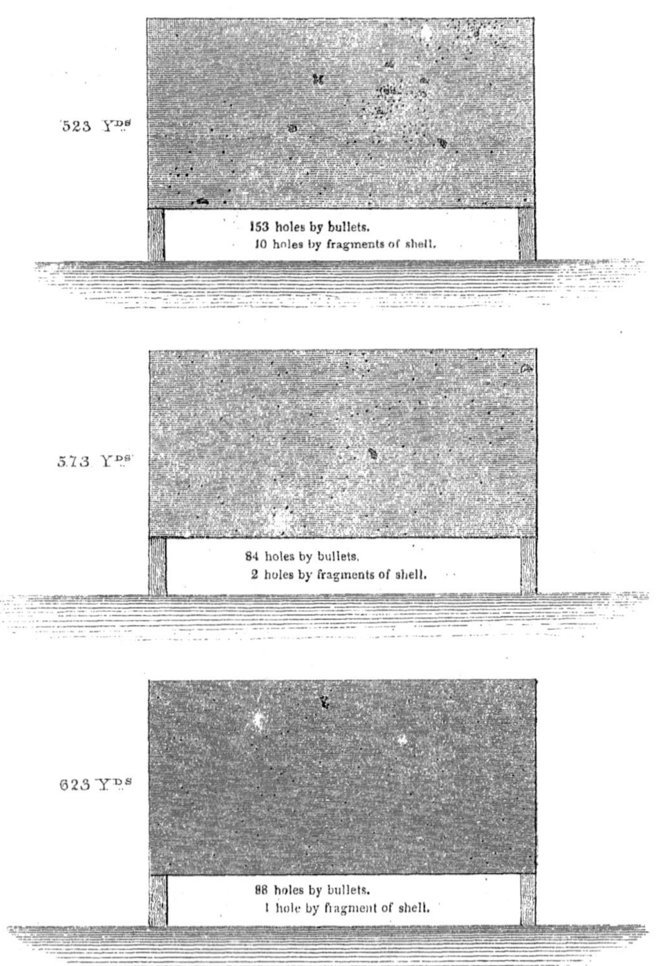

scale $\frac{1}{120}$

Dahlgren's Boat Howitzers

D. Chillas Lith. 50 S. 3d St. Phil.

CHARGE OF HOWITZER 1 lb.

No. of Rounds.	Weight of Shrapnel and Sabot.	Sight from Apex.	Time of Fuze.	Dist. of Launch from Screen,	EXPLOSION. From Launch.	EXPLOSION. In front of Screen.	EXPLOSION. Height above Water.
	lbs.	in.		yds	yds.	yds.	feet.
1	11.80	1.75	1″	466	195	271	18
2	11.80	1.75	1	485	204	281	17
3	11.79	1.75	1½	496	326	170	15
4	11.83	1.75	1¾	511	437	74	15½
5	11.73	1.75	2	527	486	41	19½
6	11.80	1.75	2¼	559	530	29	very near water.
7	11.82	2.05	2¼	549	525	24	13
8	11.81	1.95	2¼	538	534	4	7⅔
9	11.82	1.95	2¼	544	529	15	
10	11.88	2.05	2¼	553	511	42	21⅓

The co-ordinates of the explosion were obtained by the plane-table and alidade (with some additions), used for noting ranges.

One of the shrapnel (the 9th) was not seen to explode, and may have been extinguished by the water.

The 1st screen received 153 bullets and 10 fragments of shells.

The 2d screen, 84 bullets and 2 fragments, and—

The 3d screen, 88 bullets and 1 fragment.

Fifty-six of the new shrapnel and sixty-five of the kind in use, were then fired in the grounds of the U. S. Arsenal, from various pieces of the land service, which, with the 10 rounds fired from the naval boat howitzer may be stated to have resulted thus:—

	Charge of Piece.	NEW						COMMON.					
		No. Fired.	Took effect.	Doubtful.	Failed.	Premature.	Extinguished by water.	No. Fired.	Took effect.	Doubtful.	Failed.	Premature.	Extinguished by water.
Navy 12-Pdr. Boat How.	1 lb.	10	9	0	0	0	1	0	0	0	0	0	0
Army 12-Pdr. Field How.	1	10	10	0	0	0	0	10	10	0	0	0	0
" " " Gun,	2	3	3	0	0	0	0	3	3	0	0	0	0
" " " "	3	4	3	0	1	0	0	5	3	0	1	1	0
" " " "	4	19	19	0	0	0	0	17	11	2	2	2	0
" 24-Pdr. " How.	2½	10	10	0	0	0	0	10	9	0	1	0	0
" " " "	3	5	5	0	0	0	0	10	10	0	0	0	0
" " Garrison Gun,	6	5	4	0	0	0	1	10	9	0	1	0	0
		66	63		1		2	65	55	2	5	3	

There were no premature explosions with the new shrapnel,—three with the common shrapnel.

One of the new shrapnel and five of the common shrapnel failed to explode. In two instances the action of the common shrapnel was not distinct, the smoke being seen from both, but only a single jet on the water from each, which creates a suspicion that the full effect failed from some cause.

Two of the new shrapnel are stated to have been extinguished by the water; but the elevation of one of them was so disproportioned to the time of its fuze, as to make it probable that the projectile had descended too far below the surface of the water, to admit of any visible manifestation by the small charge enclosed in the shrapnel case; particularly as the distance from the observer was quite considerable.

The evident advantage of the new shrapnel as regards security, freedom from explosion in the bore, and regularity of fuze, induced Major Mordecai and myself to recommend the system to the favorable consideration of our respective departments. The results also were in favor of the certainty of the fuze to ignite and explode the charge; but this will be more fully ascertained by subsequent experience, and the officers of our Navy will soon have full opportunity to exercise their own judgment in regard to this, as well as to the general merits of the innovation upon the previous usage, as shrapnel and shells fitted in both ways will be issued for a while.

After the fabrication was begun for the

purpose of supplying the boat armament of the new ships with these shrapnel, a few were fired from time to time in order to note and check any defects of manufacture,—a very necessary precaution in all matters of ordnance, but particularly when changes are made. In so doing, the practice was executed as usual in service—the howitzer was handled and pointed with the service sight, by young seamen who, also, in firing at screens, chose such elevation and length of fuze as their observation dictated.

The following is cited as an instance of good shrapnel firing made in this way.

October 16*th*, 1855.

The first screen was about 500 yards distant,—the second, 525 yards,—the third, 550 yards,—size of screens, 20 feet by 10 feet.

Twelve shrapnel, containing a total of nearly one thousand balls, were fired from the 12-pdr. of 750 lbs., mounted on its field carriage and pointed by the service tangent sight:—

In 1st screen and its frame,	were	410	bullet holes	and	28	by fragments	of shell.
In 2d "	"	" 167	"		14	"	"
In 3d "	"	" 112	"		10	"	"

Average of each round of hits by bullets and fragments:

	Screens.	1st.	2d.	3d.	
Common shrapnel, practice, page 64,	545 yds.	18	12	6,	One did not burst.
Trial of new,	466 to 533	16	8½	9,	" "
New, Oct. 16th,	500	36	15	10,	All burst.

This practice was witnessed by His Excellency, the President of the United States, who happened at the time to be present in the Ordnance Department.

Of the fuze itself it is proper to say, that its arrangement is at once original and scientific. For 200 years we have been treading so closely in the footsteps of precedent that the ordinary time-fuzes of 1855 scarcely differ in the principle of applying a composition to graduate and convey flame to the charge of a shell, from that in vogue at Dale, in 1632. That of Colonel Bormann is a felicitous conception; it evinces a sound appreciation of the real difficulties involved in the problem, and exhibits the principle of solution in a masterly manner.

CHAPTER VIII.

CHARGES—SIGHTS.

THE charges assigned to the boat-howitzers are:—

24-pdrs.	. . .	2.00 lbs.
12-pdrs.	medium . .	1.00 "
12-pdrs.	light . .	0.625 "

The strength of the pieces would undoubtedly justify much greater charges than these; but it is by no means certain that the carriages, the fixtures, and even the frame itself of the boat, might not be injured by the severe recoil of pieces so light, and even be disabled by the continued repetition of the firing with heavier charges.

In terms of their heaviest projectiles, the weights of these pieces are thus:—

24-pdrs.	. . . .	55
12-pdrs.	medium . . .	63
12-pdrs.	light . . .	36

The severe recoil of carronades will serve as a guide to some idea of what may be safe in these light howitzers.

According to Beauchant and Adye, the weights, charges, &c., are:—

	Weight of Gun.		Charge.
	in lbs.	in shot.	lbs.
24-pdrs. carronade	1456	61	2
12-pdrs. "	654	51	1

There is an evident necessity, so far as grape and shrapnel are concerned, for the highest charges that can be used, even to one-third the weight of projectile; for, in both, the effect depends on the force given by the charge, while low charges will answer for plain shells, the action of which relies principally on the force of the powder contained in the shell; and so long as the latter is borne to the proper point, it is immaterial with what velocity it arrives there, so far as regards its final action when uncovered troops are exposed to it. But when it happens, as it often will in boat expeditions, that the enemy is protected by such quarters as small craft or merchantmen afford them, very low charges will not answer even for the plain shell of such small calibres.

So that, on the whole, the tendency is evidently towards high charges for this species of artillery; and if experience should make it sure that the fixtures in boats, and the boats themselves, will endure the action of higher charges than those assigned preliminarily, then it will be advisable to augment them. This, however, should not be done on slight grounds, or on hasty conclusions.

SIGHTS.

It seems reasonable that similar terms should be used in marking the sight and the fuze, for there is a direct and inseparable relation existing between the functions of these two agents essential to the perfect action of shrapnel. By one, the elevation is given to the piece which is required to carry the projectile to the proper distance, while the fuze adjusts the explosion to the time which the projectile occupies in traversing this space.

I am inclined, therefore, to consider the English method of marking sights as the best suited to shrapnel, inasmuch as it is the most practical, and therefore best adapted to the excitement of the action and of the actors.

The sight in this method* is graduated to the intervals of time which will carry the projectile to its desired position; and each graduation is accompanied by the two distances which include the spread of the shrapnel balls.

Thus if the fuze be adjusted to 2″, and the piece elevated by the sight, raised to the line on it marked 2″, then the shrapnel will burst about 500 yards from the piece, and spread its balls from that point to a considerable distance farther—effectively, at least 150 yards.

The sights thus graduated are only to be considered as general means to guide the intelligent officer in a proper application of shrapnel or of shells, when used upon uncovered troops; there being left in the fraction of seconds, a wide margin for the tact and discretion that are to make his fire more or less effectual.

---

* British Gunner, Adye.

CHAPTER IX.

USE OF CANISTER, SHELL, AND SHRAPNEL.

It is the common opinion and practice that grape or canister is always to be resorted to in field guns or howitzers, when uncovered masses of men are the objects of the fire, and are not beyond the distance where the dispersion of the grape, or its loss of force, renders it inefficient. This distance will vary with the piece.

It is also to be remembered that many of the balls will ricochet, and, if the surface of the soil or water be uneven, the effect of the grape will be yet more reduced in distance.

The terrible effects of grape are fully exemplified in many passages of the field of Buena Vista; particularly in the repulse of the division attacking the position held by Washington's battery; and in a yet higher degree when the reserves were concentrated by Santa

Anna, towards the close of the day. At that critical instant, the batteries of Bragg, and others, held in check a column of 5000 or 6000 men, and subsequently, assisted by the fire of the Mississippi and Indiana regiments, drove it back with great loss.

When the objects were beyond the effective play of canister, it has been customary to resort to shells, but, as already stated, it is now proposed to substitute shrapnel, and this involves the respective merits of the two projectiles, and the much-mooted question of superior fitness for the purpose in view.

In both, the due operation of the fuze is an essential element: and, therefore, no advantage can be claimed for one more than the other, as regards the *chances* of total failure or untimely action; each partakes equally in this liability.

Keeping, then, in view that uncovered men are supposed to be subjected to the fire of the howitzers, the chief points for consideration will be:—

1. The probable effect of shrapnel or shell, assuming that each explodes as desired.

The opposing force may be similarly presented to the action of these projectiles, whether disposed in columns or line in the field, or in boats pulling in line ahead or abreast.

The 12-pdr. shrapnel contains 80 musket-balls, which are dispersed from the point of explosion, with a velocity not less than that of the shrapnel at the instant. The practice already exhibited indicates the probable number of balls that would be received by the leading boats and by those astern, and the force which they retain would certainly be efficient for more than 150 yards from the explosion, while the lateral spread would include the same extent and an equal force of penetration for all the balls.

On the other hand, as the material of boats does not afford sufficient thickness for the lodgment and bursting of shell, its effect must be obtained by the dispersion of the fragments among the boat's crew or by sinking the boat; the force of these is derived from the explosion of a charge of half a pound of powder, and the number, on an average, about 12 to 13 pieces; the power of those from the posterior part of the shell will be nearly nullified by the velocity of the shell, while some must receive nearly a vertical direction, and, in returning to the surface, have little more force than that given by gravity. Many of the fragments, therefore, will fail of effect, while most of the 80 balls in the shrapnel* will

---

* I concur entirely with Captain de Brette's (note in French translation of previous Edition of this Memorandum, page 77), in regard to the complex nature of the trajectory produced by the balls and fragments of a shrapnel exploding when in motion. But I have abstained from discussing the phenomena thence arising because the intention of the Memorandum was chiefly to render a practical explanation to those concerned in the use of the system of Boat Armament that now exists in our Navy.

At some season of more leisure than the present, I hope to be able to treat more fully of the *rationale* of this and each other detail noted in this Memorandum.

There are abundant means at hand for the purpose, from the first principles and raw material, with the adjustment of the finished parts, to the application of the complete arm.

As already stated at page 62, the development of the dispersed balls and the fragments of an exploding shrapnel upon the horizontal plane beneath it, is generally ellipsoidal or ovoidal, the larger axis being in the direction of the trajectory, as one will readily detect in observing the effects upon the water. But the cone of dispersion will obviously vary with the nature of the forces whose combination produces it. That of the shrapnel which have a very small charge and a chamber to enclose it, is observed here to be much less expanded than that of the shrapnel in which the charge is greater and disseminated among the balls.

sweep the surface with a trajectory continued from that of the shrapnel, and with a velocity undiminished materially save by the resistance of the atmosphere.

These views are sustained by the results developed on the screens.

2. The difficulties which interfere with the due explosion of shell or shrapnel are common to either, and, therefore, will exert an equal influence on both.

The shell is intended to burst about the instant of first graze, or while bounding, and a timely explosion is no less essential for it than for the shrapnel; a failure in exactness, just as detrimental to its efficiency. If a column, whether of men or boats, be under fire, the shell has its whole extent for an opportunity to explode. So has the shrapnel, which, may act on the rear of the column from above, or may burst on ricochet, when it may still operate effectually. When a line is the object, the necessity of exactness in timing the explosion to the distance is just as indispensable in the shell as the shrapnel; for the want of extension of the object in the direction which the projectile takes, admits of but little variation in the time of explosion for either.

3. The consequence of exploding a shrapnel prematurely has already been shown by the practice, and it is certain that, even if it occur at 100 or 120 yards in front of the object, one-seventh of the number of balls may be relied on; under like circumstances, the fragments of a 12-pdr. shell would have been nearly harmless.

It is probable that there is little difference in the relative effect, when the explosion occurs on ricochet.

Total failures of the explosive effect must be expected with both, if the object is passed before explosion.

It may also be urged, that the shrapnel is entitled to the benefit of an opportunity to remove any doubt that may exist to its disadvantage,—while shells of light artillery are known to be held in small esteem by competent authorities, who cite the results in the field thus:—

"Experience shows that when shells burst in the air, even but a short distance from the object, they seldom reach it, and then with few fragments. Hence it is that, for some time, less importance is attached to them as a means of offence against troops, and, consequently, it might happen that shrapnel will gradually replace them entirely. The real effect of the shell as a projectile, and the moral impression produced by the menacing jet of flame from its fuze, which, by the way, is singularly diminished with veterans who have often witnessed the consequences, cannot be considered a sufficient reason for associating it with shrapnel in the equipment for the field."—(Moritz Meyer, p. 399.)

When the hostile force is sheltered, especially by such quarters as small craft or merchantmen afford, or when material of any kind is the object of the fire, then the shell can, no doubt, be advantageously substituted for shrapnel.

CHAPTER X.

DISTANCE.

WHATEVER be the circumstances under which firing is executed, or the species of projectile used, too much care cannot be taken to avoid excessive distances.

This tendency is not to be attributed to those who led the destinies of our navy in the war of 1812 and previously.

They cheerfully accepted the gauge of decisive battle from the seamen who had been trained upon the maxims of Nelson. Wherefore the point blank, expressed by the horizontal sight of that school, squared well with their wishes and convictions.

But it is generally admitted now, that the changes in ordnance that have occurred since that period will give to skill and experience the means of making gunnery effective far beyond the point blank of any piece. The views derived from observing the results of actual conflict still hold good with some, while the new opinions prevail with many. But it is much to be feared that the want of practice with shot and shells, may lead to very dangerous errors in over-estimating the range beyond which, the ordinary chances of effect are too few to be reliable.

This may, indeed, prove a most pernicious mischief, pregnant with injurious consequences, particularly as regards a just conception of the power of artillery, which, unproductive of any result when thus misapplied, shakes the faith of those who commit the error, and gives confidence to those against whom it is directed.

The effective range of field pieces (and perhaps of most other artillery) may be limited to 1200 or 1300 yards. Practice, and the common opinion of good authorities, sustain this view. For instance, the French "Aide Mémoire," issued by direction of the committee of artillery (1844), in giving the ranges of bronze cannon, appends this remark:—

"Beyond 1200 metres (1300 yards) there is little accuracy of fire, and it cannot be employed save in exceptional cases. It is only given here with the view of showing the power of the guns."

The table to which this is annexed includes the ranges, not only of such pieces as the boat-howitzer, but of 8-in. howitzers and heavy 24-pdr. cannon.

The text-book of the military school at Saint Cyr, and used also at West Point, says:—

"The fire of artillery should be delivered slowly, when the distance is greater than 600 or 700 metres, in order that it may be executed with certainty. It should cease when the enemy is at 1000 metres or 1200 metres; otherwise he may derive confidence from not sustaining any damage, and push boldly forward. Within 600 metres, the fire should be quick, being then sure; but it is only at a decisive moment that it should be as rapid as possible. By using ammunition profusely, the supply intended for a campaign may be expended in a few hours, and in the mere opening of an affair.

"We may here observe that the rate of firing should be much less than one round per minute, for, the double allowance of an 8-pdr. being 416 rounds, it will be perceived that, by firing once a minute, the whole supply for a campaign will be consumed in seven hours. It is admitted that rapid firing should only be resorted to in some particular cases; and that, generally, it should be executed slowly, so as to make certain, by its accuracy, of producing the greatest effect with the least amount of ammunition.

Manuel de l'Artilleur, by GENERAL DURTUBIE, p. 8.—"But at these elevations (3° and 6°) ammunition is always expended uselessly, because, with long guns as well as with short guns, accuracy is not to be had at too great ranges; and, therefore, noise is made at a manifest loss. In the use of the field-piece, too, the greatest elevation is not beyond two and a half degrees."

Traité d'Artillerie, by COLONEL PIOBERT, p. 421.—"To produce a good effect, the firing should not be performed at a greater angle than 2° above the ground. Aim directly, but a little low, at distances which do not exceed 900 or 1000 metres; beyond these, fire on ricochet, and at an angle of 1° to

1600 or 1700 metres—which are the limits of this species of practice on the most favorable ground."

Ibid. p. 422.—"The firing should not be too hasty nor too rapid, especially if there be no certainty of being able to replace the ammunition immediately, or of producing a very advantageous effect."*

Fortunately there is a corrective to this evil, so far as regards the shells and shrapnel of such pieces as these howitzers, which cannot be easily avoided. The duration of their longest fuzes does not exceed 5 seconds of time, and therefore cannot be employed beyond the distances corresponding thereto, which happen not to surpass the extreme limit. It is advisable, however, to make use of this time very seldom. Not only do the difficulties interpose that arise from the distance corresponding thereto and which are applicable to any kind of projectile, but, with shrapnel, the ellipse of the dispersion is much contracted on its greater axis. The 5″ fuze

---

* The pieces here spoken of are field-pieces, and have greater ranges and greater power than howitzers can have.

of the ordinary kind, is also the least certain of receiving and retaining ignition, as all such fuzes are, in which the composition is weakened in order to give the time; the length being limited by the construction of the shrapnel, which requires the fuze to be kept free from the balls, that would otherwise bruise or break it.

This latter objection does not, of course, apply to the Bormann fuze, for its composition is of equal strength throughout.

PLATE 9.

PIVOTS AND TRAVERSES FOR BOW OF FRIGATE LAUNCH

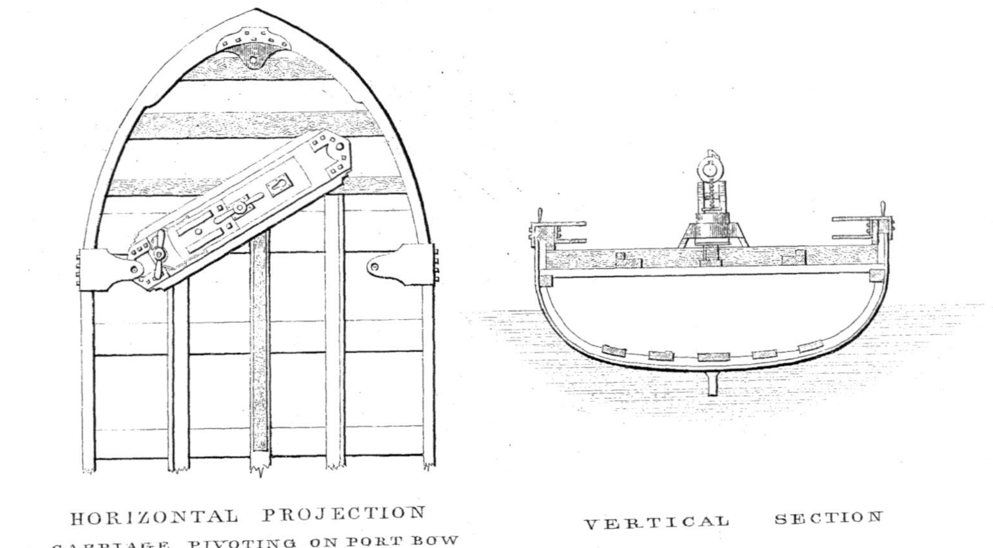

HORIZONTAL PROJECTION
CARRIAGE PIVOTING ON PORT BOW

VERTICAL SECTION

D.Chillas Lith. 86 S.5 St. Phil

CHAPTER XI.

EQUIPMENT OF BOAT.

The appliances for mounting the howitzers in boats, the manner of working them, embarking and disembarking, &c., will perhaps be best comprehended by a description of a Frigate's launch, fitted for actual service, which has been used in the experimental practice.

This boat is 34½ feet in length, and has an extreme beam of 11¼ feet; built and finished in all respects as usual in service.

The boat-carriage should be so placed in the bow as to carry the muzzle of the howitzer just above and clear of the gunwale and stem. Two pieces of yellow pine are laid athwart-ship, so as to bear the carriage at this height, and on them it traverses when pivoted at the stem. The warping chocks at the stem and stern-post should not be permanent fixtures, but be arranged so as to be movable when the gun is used. The two iron plates for receiving the slide are welded into one piece, which is firmly bolted beneath the breast-hook of the bow.

When pivoting on the stem or stern-plates, the howitzer has the sweep permitted by the form of the boat; about a point and a half either way if forward, and considerable more if aft. Two pivot-plates are bolted on each bow so that the howitzer may be trained more or less on the beam; the stem-plates being adjusted first and the carriage fitted in.

The distances between the bolt of the stem-plate and that of either bow-pivot must be equal to the distances between the holes in each end of the slide, and the pivot-bolts of the two bow-plates also correspond to the same distance. The pivots are thus at the points of an equilateral triangle, which enables a rapid and certain management of the gun in changing its position.

Thus, if the gun be pivoted at the stem, it is brought to either bow by bolting the rear of the slide on one bow, taking out the stem pivot-bolt, and training the fore end to the

PLATE 10

FRIGATES LAUNCH.

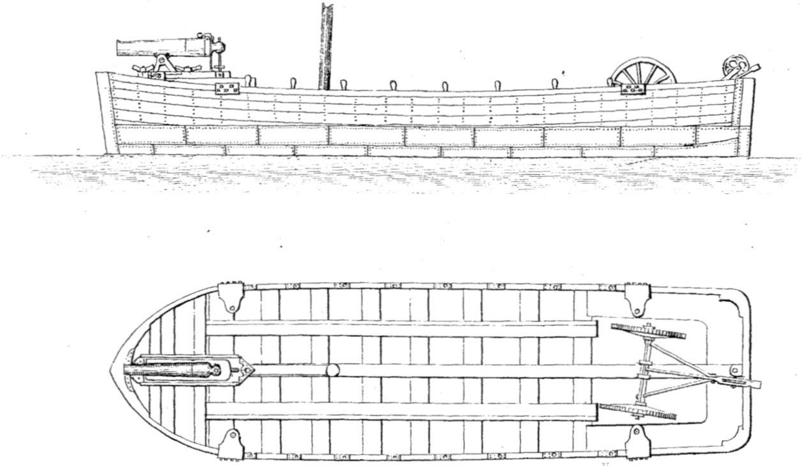

D. Chillas Lith. 50 S. 3 St. Phil.

opposite bow. If it be pivoted on the one bow, it can be used on the opposite bow by bolting the rear of the slide to the pivot-plate on that side, and reversing the gun and its bed on the slide. To sustain the carriage in sweeping, when pivoted to the bow, a piece of yellow pine scantling is placed lengthwise and amidship, mortised into the rear cross-piece.

The arrangements for the stern are to be adapted to the same principle, and the management of the piece will always be found more convenient in the stern-sheets than bow, as the construction of the boat gives so much more space there.

If a landing is likely to be necessary, the field-carriage is placed forward or aft, according to circumstances. If in the stern-sheets, the wheels are to be down on the platform and the trail laid over the quarter. In landing, the boat will be laid bow or stern off, as may be required by the wind and sea. Two light wooden tracks are laid along the thwarts for the wheels, and one amidship for the trail. Eye-bolts are driven into the bow and stern to receive the hooks of two stout skids, which are connected at the outer end by hooking an iron brace.

When the launch is beached, which, of course, would only be done in a tolerably smooth time, two men jump overboard, each drawing one skid along, and are assisted in hooking them to the bow by two of the men in the boat. Meanwhile, the field-carriage has been lifted to the tracks and run forward to the gun, the elevating screw of which has been removed, and a block placed on the slide, so that the muzzle of the piece may rest on it. A small selvagee strap is passed through the breeching-hole, or around the neck of the pomilion, and a spar put through it. The loop-bolt is withdrawn; two men at each end of the spar lift up the breech of the gun high enough to permit the wheels of the field-carriage to go clear beneath; which is done until the lugs of the axle are under the loop of the gun; then lower down and bolt it; screw in the elevator.

It will often happen in swaying up the piece that it will turn round a little, so that, when lowered, the loop will not enter fairly into the lugs. The difficulty is easily prevented by thrusting through the breeching-hole a short iron or wooden bolt, by which the piece is slued fair in a moment.

Eight or ten men now jump overboard, and those who remain in, run the gun over the bow on the skids, easing it down by the drag-rope secured to the trail. The men outboard are to keep outside the skids, and moderate the descending movement by bearing up against the spokes. When upon the bottom, slue the piece round and run it up out of the water.

The time required in a launch to shift the 12-pdr. from its boat-carriage to the field-carriage ought not to exceed forty-five seconds; it is commonly done in less time, and even in thirty seconds, when the men work correctly. The time of disembarkation will depend entirely on circumstances. With a good beach, smooth water, and a well-drilled crew, it should never exceed two minutes.

The following are from memoranda of practice at this yard:—

The beach, at high water, afforded fair footing, but not altogether of the best kind. The launch was pulled briskly up to it, the piece fired at the instant of touching, shifted to its field-carriage, landed, run well up on the shore, wheeled and fired.

At the first trial, the time, from fire to fire, was *three minutes.*

At the second trial, *two minutes.*

The results of the third trial are thus stated in the memorandum made on the spot:—

Monday, June 9th, 1851.

Commodore Warrington, Chief of Bureau of Ordnance, and Commodore Morris, Inspector of Ordnance, (lately deceased as Chief of the Bureau), attended by Commodore Ballard, the Commandant of the Navy Yard, embarked in the launch to examine the arrangements for the boat armament.

Shoved off from the wharf about noon, and pulled about half a mile into the stream.

12-pdr. of 750 lbs. in the bow. Opened with shrapnel; the launch head on. Sight 2 in. and 2.2 in. Fuze 2″.

After firing eight rounds, laid the boat broadside-to, the howitzer pivoting on port bow. Sight 1 in. and 1.2 in. Fuzes 1″. Then laid the piece point blank, at the direction of Commodore Morris, so as to try the effect on ricochet.

Pulled in for the beach, and disembarked.

Primer fired on touching the beach. Shifted the howitzer from its boat-carriage to the field-carriage. Landed the gun. Each of the men having a round in his pouch, moved up about thirty yards from the water, wheeled, and fired a primer—the houses and people not permitting the piece to be discharged.

Time elapsed from primer to primer in disembarking, 1 *minute*, 42 *seconds.*

Re-embarked, going through the same manœuvres reversed.

Time elapsed from primer to primer in re-embarking, 1 *minute*, 52 *seconds.**

---

* It is sometimes intimated, and not unreasonably, that in this, as in other cases, where occasions are selected more favorable for operations than the ordinary course of service admits of, the result cannot be assumed as a proper standard: but an instance just under notice goes to show that the practice here cited is by no means extraordinary. In the stated official Report (Dec. 17, 1855) to the Bureau of Ordnance, by Captain Bailey of the U. S. Ship St. Mary's, it is said, "In landing the 12-pdr. howitzer (of 430 lbs.) the following time was made, viz.: From the time the launch struck the beach, gun shifted from boat to field-carriage, landed and

As a pendant to this, may be given an instance when the bottom was bad, and, through carelessness, a part of the equipment defective. The coxswain reported an eye-bolt broken from the bow (used to hook the skids) just as the launch was about to shove off. It was too late to be repaired, and the chances for a lesson very good.

On beaching, the men jumped overboard as usual. The mud was soft enough to let them well down, so that the water rose above their waists, and sticky enough to embarrass their movements. With all the care that could be used, the eye-bolt left in the port-bow was insufficient to steady the skid, and it canted when the gun was half-way. The left wheel run off and fell down into the mud. It was

---

in readiness to fire, in 1 minute and 30 sec.—in 2 min. 47 sec.—in 1 min. 25 sec.—in 59 sec.—in 1 min. 12 sec.—in 1 min. 20 sec., and in 58 sec.

"Embarked in 1 min. and 45 sec.—Landed in 1 min. and 20 sec. Embarked, mounted on carriage, (boat) and fixed a primer in 45 sec. The launch and howitzer were under the command of Acting Master J. E. Jewett."

This very creditable practice is as rapid, or even more so, than that given in the text; the latter being performed, however, with the heavier piece.

not possible to lift so great a weight in such a position, and by hand. The trail, therefore, was turned right over towards the shore; this brought the gun under. The right wheel, being up on the skid, was then turned over, which brought the gun up with its trail in shore. Hooked on the drag-rope, but, so tenacious was the blue mud, that the force of all hands (16 men) was just sufficient to drag the piece up on the beach, though the wheels traversed freely. Large lumps of mud fell from the gun and carriage as it moved. This occupied about twenty minutes. The piece, however, was all right, the ammunition pouches dry, and everything ready for action. In returning, the operation was not delayed by any accident, the mud alone extending the time to seven minutes. That set of men will probably never suffer again for want of an eye-bolt in the bow.

It seems preferable, in landing, not to separate any gun from its field-carriage, as it is not only more difficult to handle the piece without it, but also exposes the gun to being bruised by dragging it along the bottom.

When the water is rough, and so much

motion in the boat as to make it hazardous to the men to trust the piece on skids, it can be mounted on its field-carriage, and lashed or slung over the gunwale of the boat before leaving the ship. When as near the beach as the surf will admit, make fast a stout line to the trail, which send ashore; cut the lashing, and lower down the piece carefully so as to land with its wheels on the bottom; the men can now drag it up on the beach.

It may be much better than this, however, to use rafts, when the water is not sufficiently smooth to run the piece on skids from the boat. The usual resources of a ship will ordinarily furnish abundant materials for this purpose; and from them it will be no difficult task for seamen to construct rafts fully suitable to the occasion.

It has been suggested that the tracks laid on the thwarts to bear the wheels of the field-carriage, may be fitted so as to hook at the bow, and thus serve in lieu of the skids placed there by which the gun is to be transferred from the boat to the beach; but any such economy of means is not to be recommended at a time requiring the utmost promptness of movement. In one case, when this arrangement had been followed, the tracks extended so far forward, that, if removed to be placed outside from the bow, the field-carriage would meanwhile have been left without any means of support. Another device connected the landing skids by a joint with the tracks, so as to fold over, without taking into account the impossibility that ensues of working the howitzer on its boat-carriage in the bow.

All that can be said in regard to the landing of guns from a boat is, that in smooth water it can be done without much trouble; but that in a surf, there is no way but to get the piece over the gunwale and ease it to the bottom with a slip rope. This has been already premised in the foregoing description of the means proposed.

In undertaking to alter the arrangements in the boats, by which the howitzers are to be handled when mounted on the boat-carriage, transferred from it to the field-carriage and then landed, it is to be borne in mind that certain conditions are imperative:—

1st. The means used must be strong and operative with the greatest ease and promptness.

2d. They must be readily placed and dis placed, as the boats which carry guns are stowed in nests on the spar-deck.

3d. They should be so simple, that when lost or damaged, they may be renewed by one of the Carpenter's crew, and from the ordinary supply of lumber which every ship has usually on hand.

It will be found on examination, that these requirements have been closely looked to in the fixtures devised. They are coarse, strong, and simple,—have no permanent connection with the boat, and are removable readily,—while the howitzer is handled with greater ease, commands a wider sweep than in any previous plan, and is disembarked with as little exertion as can be expected in such an operation.

CHAPTER XII.

SUGGESTIONS FOR LANDING.

When it becomes necessary to resort to the boats of a squadron to effect any purpose, it is evident that much will depend on the previous training of the men.

If such an occasion should be the first in which they have seen the howitzers hoisted into the boats, it may be taken for granted that they know nothing of their management, and can hardly be expected to use them intelligently or efficiently.

And should any operation result unfavorably, in which the light howitzers have borne a share, neither men nor officers engaged in the affair can be chargeable with blame, when so efficient an auxiliary has been rendered comparatively useless, for want of previous training.

To avoid conclusions so mortifying, it

would be well that some exercising should be executed frequently, until the men are conversant with every detail, and, as often afterwards as may seem requisite to keep this fresh in remembrance. Most especially in view of any demand for boat service.

The launch should be hoisted out, and fitted completely with the howitzer, ammunition, &c.; a regular system of manœuvre should then be pursued in shifting the gun to the several pivots, firing a number of blank rounds, or if a mark can be had, using shell and shrapnel; then transferring the gun to its field-carriage, and if a beach is at hand, disembarking it.

The ammunition and equipment of the piece must also be examined at due intervals, particularly to see that the primers, fuzes, and the charges of powder attached to the shell, &c., have not sustained injury from moisture or insects. The boat-carriage, when first shipped, may need slight adjustment, as exposure to the weather will cause it to warp, so that the surfaces are not correctly in contact, or the guide in the slot may have swelled. The remedy for both is easily applied, if taken in time. The nuts of the field-carriage should always be kept well screwed up, and those which secure the ends of the braces outside the axle are to have particular attention.

When the opportunity occurs for actual service, the officer selected to command the launch must have with him another officer to take charge of the howitzer, and a quarter-gunner to look after and serve the ammunition. As soon as the other boats are hoisted out of the launch, the traversing pieces for the boat-carriage are to be placed and cleated, the pivot plates bolted on the stem, stern, bows and quarters. If there be a field-carriage, the tracks are to be laid and bolted to the thwarts; the skids laid fore and aft, so as not to interfere with the pulling; the muzzle-block, selvagee for cascable, and spar for shifting the gun, disposed of conveniently, before the launch is hoisted out.

Meanwhile, the ammunition and pouches are to be brought on deck and examined carefully. The shells and shrapnel of the common description may now receive their charges of powder, which are—

	Shrapnel.	Shell.
	oz.	lbs.
For the 12-pdr. . .	4½	0.5
For the 24-pdr. . .	6	1.0

The chargers are adapted to these quantities. In filling shrapnel, only a little is to be poured in at a time, and well shaken down, until the whole charge is below the fuze-plug, then close the orifice of the plug with a tow-stopper.

Is is indifferent how many shells are charged, because it is easy to withdraw the powder, after the return to the ship, from such as have not been used. But this operation is very troublesome with the common shrapnel, and, therefore, it is advisable to charge no more than will probably be required for the service. Powder should never be suffered to remain in such shrapnel, because the motion of the balls gradually pulverizes the grain, separation of the components follows, and the charge, assumed to be already reduced to the lowest quantity that will fracture the shrapnel-case, becomes too feeble to perform its function.

The new shrapnel are free from this objection, as they are fitted and fuzed when supplied to ships,—the charge being separated from the balls, which are also prevented from moving, is not liable to be pulverized.

Spare primers may be taken from the stock of the heavy guns and some match rope. A key, for unscrewing the boxes, must be secured to the becket of each. If spare sponges are to be had, take them and see that they are used fully. The drag-rope for the field carriage should be stout, and furnished with the proper number of handles.

Every thing being conveniently stowed, and the boat properly manned, and otherwise equipped, is ready to shove off.

Supposing that a force is to be landed, the operation should be conducted under the most favorable circumstances that can be chosen, and it should be borne in mind that, in all probability, the greatest disadvantage of all is to disembark when opposed with any firmness: for, in using all the celerity that is practicable and with the best trained men, there must be a few minutes when the pieces to be put ashore are inactive, and the force thus employed is not only fairly exposed to a deliberate fire, but unable to make any return.

A very inferior force may, at such a crisis, disable a large number of men, even if it fail to repel the landing force, and may thus embarrass the forward movement to a very material extent; for, besides losing the services of those who are wounded, some must be left to attend them.

The difficulty of landing when opposed, even by an inconsiderable force, is illustrated by an example that occurred during the last century (1758), when an expedition was sent from England against the French colonies in North America. The force assigned to besiege Louisbourg was 12,000 men, while the French garrison numbered about 3200. The historian states that—

"The governor had taken all the precaution in his power to prevent the landing, by establishing a chain of posts that extended two leagues and a half along the most accessible parts of the beach. Intrenchments were thrown up and batteries erected, but *there were some intermediate places* which could not be properly secured, and in one of these the English troops were disembarked."

* * * * *

"On the 8th day of June, the troops being assembled in the boats before daybreak, in three divisions, several sloops and frigates, that were stationed along shore, in the bay of Gabarus, began to scour the beach with their shot; and, after the fire had continued about a quarter of an hour, the boats containing the division on the left,* were rowed towards the shore under the command of Brigadier-General Wolfe, an accomplished officer, who, in the sequel, displayed very extraordinary proofs of military genius. At the same time, the two other divisions, on the right and in the centre, commanded by the Brigadiers Whitmore and Laurence, made a show of landing, in order to divide and distract the enemy. Notwithstanding an impetuous surf, by which many boats were overset, and a very severe fire of cannon and musketry from the enemy's batteries, which did considerable execution, Brigadier Wolfe pursued his point with admirable courage and deliberation. The soldiers leaped into the water with the most eager alacrity, and, gaining the shore, attacked the

* Grenadiers, light infantry, and Frazer's Highlanders.

enemy in such a manner that, in a few minutes, they abandoned their works and artillery, and fled in the utmost confusion."—(SMOLLETT'S *History of England*, II. 387.)

It will be noticed that:—

1. The British force was vastly superior to the French, who necessarily could spare but a small part of the garrison to defend the landing.

2. There were intermediate places not properly secured, and probably could not be for want of men. Here the English troops disembarked.

3. The division was composed of the best troops, and led by the heroic Wolfe.

The only disadvantages were a considerable surf, and a rocky shore, reached, in some measure, by the cannon of the nearest intrenchments.

And yet these were so nearly able to counterbalance the immense superiority of the attacking force, that General Wolfe, in a private letter to Colonel Rickson, remarks:—

"Amongst ourselves, be it said, that our attempt to land where we did, was rash and injudicious, our success unexpected (by me) and undeserved. There was no prodigious exertion of courage in the affair; *an officer and thirty men would have made it impossible to get ashore where we did.* Our proceedings in other respects were as slow and tedious as this undertaking was ill-advised and desperate; but this for your private information only."

A very significant commentary on the chances to which an expedition is exposed in attempting to land in a surf in the face of an enemy, especially when it is remembered that no officer would have been more likely to command success, in such an enterprize, than the intrepid young general who led the men in person. He not long afterwards ended his bright career at Quebec, at the early age of thirty-two.

In perusing the letter of Wolfe, one is led to note how slight the chance on which success depended, and how easily the brilliant picture of the general historian might have been converted into a very dismal sketch, by reverses in a matter so trifling to him, and his authority, as seemingly to be beneath their notice.

Judicious means, therefore, must be used to get the expedition ashore without opposition; avoiding it either by keeping out of sight, or, if seen, by pulling rapidly to some point which can be more readily reached by the boats than by the party ashore, or by dividing the force, and making false attacks upon several points.

If, however, such attempts are unavailing, then it only remains to land promptly in the face of the enemy, and, to this end, that part of the beach must be selected where the footing is most likely to be firm, the bank gradually shelving, and the bottom freest from rocks and stones, least exposed to the surf, and, most especially, where no cover of any kind for the enemy exists within some hundred yards of the shore, and consequently nothing to protect them from the free play of the guns.

Rafts may afford the best means of landing field-pieces in the surf. These are readily put together on shipboard with spare spars, gratings, &c., buoyed by gang-casks, breakers, &c.

The pieces are mounted on their field-carriages with the ammunition-boxes at the axles well provided against wet, and secured so as not to start with the motion of the rafts. The seamen attached to the piece accompany it with their pouches slung and a round in each. Two stout grapnels are stowed on the rafts.

The boats and rafts, which carry the landing force, should be in the middle of the line. The covering launches, carrying the 24-pdr. howitzers, should be placed at each extremity of the line, and somewhat in advance, so as to be in position before the landing force is near the shore. Generally, it will be best for them to come within good canister range of the beach, say 200 to 300 yards, or even nearer.

The disposition of the covering force is of the greatest importance; it should be so arranged as to give free scope to the advance of the other boats while it operates against the shore until the landing is fairly established.

At the proper time, the whole force pulls in for the designated landing, according to the plan of the commanding officer,—the rafts towed in by the most powerful boats.

If there be a surf running, the rafts and

launches will let go their grapnels outside of it; taking such positions as will enable each to perform a proper part, and veering in as desired. As the boats swing round, the covering launches will open on whatever may be sufficiently near to molest the landing force.

The rafts with the field-pieces now veer rapidly, so as to approach the shore; and the moment they touch, the men run the pieces on the beach, previously loaded with canister, if the position is critical and the enemy within a short distance; otherwise, they load after landing, according to circumstances.

Meanwhile the other boats dash at the shore, and when near enough to it, the marines and seamen jump into the water, muskets loaded and bayonets fixed, and are disposed so as to suit the emergency. If the enemy crowd down to meet the boats, the howitzer forward may send a round or two of canister among them, immediately previous to the men leaving the boat.

At this important moment all will depend on the activity and training of the seamen, acting as infantry, and the rapid perception of the officers who *lead* them. In handling the howitzers, coolness and precision *only* are required; not a round must be lost; and great care by the covering launches used, to avoid injuring one's own people as they approach the enemy.

It will be seen that if the opposing force attempts to close with the landing party, its line is taken obliquely by the 24-pdr. howitzers; and, if not checked by this, they will in a few minutes be encountered by an additional play of canister from the field howitzers and the musketry.

The first measure of the force disembarked is to move rapidly forward to fulfil the object of the expedition. The crew of each piece carrying one or two pouches with fixed charges and ammunition chests lashed under the axles, if required.

The people in the boats will at once prepare to receive the men who are ashore, when they shall return. The boats or rafts, which have been beached, must therefore be floated, hauled out, and held by a grapnel head off, veering in as far as may be convenient.

Clothes-bags, bread-bags, or barrels, filled

with sand or earth, and piled up, will constitute a ready and defensible barricade; and, with a howitzer or two, will make a good rallying point, and cover a re-embarkation or reinforcement.

Suitable arrangements should always be made for re-embarking, and demand even more care, in selecting the proper spot and in giving security to the operation, than for disembarking; because the failure in this case will be far more disastrous, as it will compromise the lives of many men, and may cause the capture of the whole, as well as of the boats thus left without sufficient numbers to defend them; whereas the repulse of an attempt to disembark need not involve the loss of the party.

An instance of what may result from not properly providing for re-embarkation, is shown in the following account of an expedition which the English landed on the French coast in 1758.

"The Bay of St. Cas was covered by an entrenchment which the enemy had thrown up, to prevent or oppose any disembarkation; and on the outside of this work there was a range of sand hills extending along shore, which could have served as a cover to the enemy, from whence they might have annoyed the troops in re-embarking: for this reason a proposal was made to the general that the forces should be re-embarked from a fair open beach on the left, between St. Cas and Guildo; but this advice was rejected."

The rear guard of 1500 men was attacked by the French, and 1000 killed or taken, including General Drury, although the fire from the frigates seems to have swept the ground very destructively.

The historian follows the account of this expedition with some remarks, and says:—

"Should it be judged expedient, however, to prosecute this desultory kind of war, the commanders employed in it will do well to consider that a descent ought never to be hazarded in an enemy's country, without having taken proper precautions to secure a retreat; that the severest discipline ought to be preserved during all the operations of the campaign, that a general ought never to disembark, but on a well-concerted plan, nor commence his military transactions without some immediate point or object in view; that a re-embarkation ought never to be attempted, except from a clear, open beach, where the approaches of an enemy may be seen, and the troops covered by the fire of their shipping." —(SMOLLETT'S *History of England*, II., 378.)

In all expeditions where it may be necessary to act ashore as well as afloat, it will be found that the 12-pdr. of 750 lbs. unites more advantages in this two-fold capacity than almost any other howitzer. For landing, and for movements over ground with a good stock of ammunition, it has the decided advantage of the 24-pdr., which, from its own weight and that of the ammunition, would frequently be unmanageable. And, as regards range and power, it is far above comparison with the light 12-pdr.

As artillerymen, good seamen are not easily excelled, and, therefore, in maintaining a position, may be fully relied on to do so, as long as the means furnished permit. A memorable instance of their capacity in this way occurred at the battle of Bladensburg, where choice British infantry were unable to carry, by a front attack, the pieces manned by Commodore Barney and his sailors, and were forced to effect their purpose by a flank movement.

Their habits and training, however, do not fit them for manœuvring with facility, or in compact order; and it would be unwise, therefore, to expose them voluntarily to measure force in the field with disciplined infantry. Whenever necessity should lead to such a measure, it should be based on the unquestioned superiority of the sailors, in numbers and appointments; and all the marines should accompany the expedition.

It is important, in coming under fire with a division of boats, that they should not pull in line ahead towards it; and if in line abreast, that they should be so far asunder as not to permit the scattering of canister or shrapnel to cover more than one boat. Otherwise, it will hardly be possible to avoid suffering from every round. The fire of the whole line should, on the other hand, be concentrated on the principal masses of the enemy.

The admonition given by a good authority*

* Instr. d'Artill.

for the *general* service of artillery, will be found particularly applicable to that of the boat armament.

"To develope the full effect of artillery, its fire should be delivered at good range, with coolness and judgment; every impetuous outbreak of mere courage being forbidden."

In all the details of ordnance, large and small, there has been vast improvement of *material*, since the first introduction, but no corresponding advance in the training and practice of the *personal;* precipitate, and ill-timed firing is just as common now as it was in the most primitive epochs of artillery, and unfortunately most of the inventive power of the present day tends rather to increase than to diminish this evil.

Every battle can furnish its full share of the mischief produced by the indiscriminate firing of artillery, though the fact may not always be recorded. Here is a case where inexperience could not be assigned as an excuse:—

"About 8 o'clock, the enemy's columns began to pass the fords (of the Bidassoa), covered by the fire of their artillery; but the first shells thrown fell into the midst of their own ranks, and the British troops on Santa Barbara cheered the French battery with a derisive shout."—(Napier, IV. 222.)

Sometimes entire defeat has resulted from this seemingly incorrigible vice.

Wherefore, however *excellent* the skill of the officers, and the training of the men, there is a *limit to the rapidity* with which the fire of artillery should be executed; beyond this, *no certainty can be expected, and the results must be those of the merest chance.*

CHAPTER XIII.

HINTS FOR GENERAL SERVICE.

THE points of chief interest in relation to the proper condition and management of boat armament, may be briefly condensed as follows:—

FOR PROJECTILES.

The wooden plug to receive the fuze of common shrapnel or shells, must be examined to see that it is free from cracks, and a gauge inserted into the orifice, to be certain that its dimensions have not been altered.

See if the sabot be sound, and that the tacks hold the straps firmly.

If the charge is not attached or fixed to the

PLATE 11.

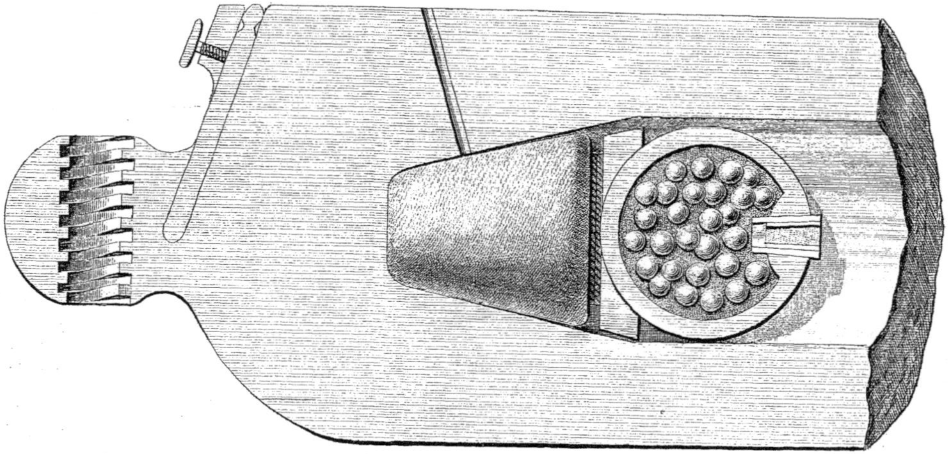

SECTION OF BOAT HOWITZER.

D. Chillas Lith. 50 S. 3. St. Phil.

sabot of the projectile, have it properly done, as it simplifies the operation of loading, which is most desirable in action.

If already fixed, examine the twine which secures the cylinder to the sabot, and see that the knotting remains good; feel if the charge have caked, or if there be any appearance of moisture about the flannel cylinder, or perforations by insects. If powder dust should have filtered through, brush it entirely away: premature explosion may arise from a neglect to do this.

Imperfection in any of these particulars should be remedied immediately; and, if necessary, the round taken apart and refixed.

AMMUNITION.

The primer, to be in good order, should have the barrel of the quill free from splits: the joint where the wafer is connected with the quill sound, and the shellac adhering there and on the whole wafer; and particularly the tipping at the end of the quill, intended to keep the moisture from the charge therein, and to prevent small grains from dropping out.

If the paper covering of the common fuzes is unbroken, and the shellac coating not cracked, the fuzes themselves are probably in good order.

The boxes containing the ammunition should be close at the joints, and perfectly tight when the lid is screwed down.

EQUIPMENT.

Examine the equipments of the howitzer; the lock and sight should move freely and truly; the laniard be sound, and the elevating screw clean, but no hard rubbing ever permitted in order to make it bright; the thread is worn by it, and the screw will cease to prevent the jumping of the breech in firing—a very important consideration. At sea, the continued motion of the ship will tend to create this defect; therefore, the elevator should ordinarily be removed and the breech of the gun supported by a block of wood.

Do not lose sight of the sponge; a good one is a prime essential in service.

Look after the appliances for shifting the howitzer from one carriage to another; the block for the muzzle, the strap for the pomilion, and the spar, which also is to serve for the socket in the trail of the field-carriage, so as to point the piece.

The boat-carriage is to be examined carefully; it must work freely when not compressed; and be as firm as if it were one piece, when the compressors are set hard. In correcting the errors incident to warping, be careful to remove but very slight shavings; two small buttons underneath the lower plate prevent the bolts from dropping down when the compression is relieved; they cannot be dispensed with. Take care that grease is never applied to the surfaces of the slide or bed; the compressors in that case will not control the recoil. The carriage should be protected from the rain and sun when not in service.

It is advisable not to take the field-carriage apart: nuts and pins may be lost through some of the many contingencies of sea-service, and then trouble and delay will occur, when perhaps it may be most desirable that all should move with the greatest dispatch. Examine the nuts occasionally; they should be firmly screwed; those which hold the braces outside of the axle will demand particular attention.

When the pivot-plates are removed from the launch, so as to stow the other boats, they and their bolts and nuts should be tallied and stowed in the store-room, the wooden traverses for the boat-carriage, the tracks and skids for the field-carriage put away safely and where they will be at hand. Look out for the eye-bolts in the bow and stern, to which the skids are to be hooked.

A rope or chain may be provided to lock the wheels in descending slopes of much inclination.

In short, too much care cannot be taken to be fully provided and to have each detail in good condition: for after the boat has left the ship, it may be impossible to compensate for failure in some seemingly trivial article. Captain Paynter very correctly observes in his "Notes on Boat Service," (p. 15):

"I consider that if a ship can, by her discipline, send her boats away for distant service in 15 minutes, and one of them be found deficient in any particular, she forfeits all claim to be considered before a ship that is an hour in her evolution, but has "every thing that human foresight can consider requisite for all the exigencies of service."

In serving the howitzer, the practice here has always been to moisten the sponge, and though it differs from that common in the land service, there seems to be much to recommend it; especially in this, that the least trace of fire must be extinguished.

In the course of six years' operations with these howitzers in every variety of rapid and slow firing, no accident has yet occurred from premature explosion.

In firing, *never* jerk the laniard; having just strain enough to straighten it, draw with a sharp, quick blow, and continue the force until the hammer is felt to be down. Perhaps in a thousand primers not more than four or five will fail, whether it rain or shine, provided the water does not reach the charge. The primer will go through the flannel without pricking.

Never fire faster than you can aim fairly, and surely; and in view of the tendencies to random shooting, still so prevalent, it would be well, in service as well as in exercising, to pause after aiming, and give a chance for another look at the object. When you see those objects closing on you, at a couple of hundred yards, then lay your gun point blank for the ground at their feet; and if you can make six or seven discharges in the minute that follows, so much the better. *At such times canister only is wanted.*

Eight rounds per minute have often been fired here from the 12-pdr. of 750 lbs. on its field-carriage, — and more frequently four rounds, in times varying from 15 seconds to 18 seconds.

If the piece must retain position, two men of a side, by taking hold of the spokes, will check the recoil and run the piece up to its place. On rough, or soft ground, the trail should be carried in recoil by its wheel or runner; but not when the ground is smooth and firm.

It has been the common practice on ship board to brighten the boat howitzers which, however ornamental, will be found very inconvenient in service, as the brilliant reflection of the sun's rays must dazzle the best sight and interfere seriously in aiming.—It also discloses the presence, positions, and movements of the guns far beyond gunshot, and thus furnishes information to an adversary which he may turn to his own account. The proper color is the dark green, commonly known as bronze, which is generally not disliked, and this will be acquired with some rapidity under the influence of sea-air. At first the formation of the light green deposit may not be very sightly, but with some little care this need not last long.

CONCLUSION

AND

RESULTS OF ACTUAL SERVICE.

The application of a naval force to the purposes of littoral warfare can only be considered as incidental to the general purposes for which a navy is created, and the character of such operations is necessarily limited by that of the force, and by its strength. The squadrons which the navy might collect from its present number of ships would seldom be able to land a sufficient number of seamen to admit of acting, excepting as subsidiaries, against the forts, posts, or detachments that would be found along the shores of any civilized nation at war with us, even admitting that the adaptation to the field, of the force landed, was equal to that which could be opposed to it.

Thus, it does not frequently happen that either the *personal* or *material* of war can be reached to any important extent by parties from our ships; and when they have been employed by any of the maritime powers of

Europe against each other or against the United States, their operations have been desultory, and often followed by deplorable evils. Our own maritime expeditions in the war with Mexico, with hardly an exception, fully attained the end proposed in each case, while humanity and a due sense of individual rights were observed by all; yet the navy may well deprecate any course of events which is calculated to withdraw it from its legitimate sphere of action on the broad Ocean, where it may protect the commerce of the country, and oppose itself fairly to the armed force of the enemy. Here it may win honor and effect great results.

Exceptional cases, however, occur where the strength of a ship or a squadron may be landed with important effect. Such occurred in California in the recent war, and there are others, where the rights of the flag, of civilization, or of humanity, enforce the necessity of using a sea force for the want of other means. The offences of savage nations or islanders, and of a piratical people, may be cited as cases requiring punishment or intimidation.

It is also within the proper scope of a navy to render assistance in the disembarkation of a land force; and, on these occasions, the boat howitzers may be useful in covering the troops; while in attacking small craft, such pieces will be indispensable. During 1823, in the West Indies, and subsequently in the Grecian Archipelago, the cruizing boats from the squadrons would have been materially aided, had they been provided with howitzers.

In the defence of our own shores and homesteads, sailors are in all respects proper and valuable auxiliaries. Wherefore, when the public service requires the ships of war to disembark the men, it is believed that these howitzers will be found serviceable, if used properly; not omitting to remember that their capacity is also unequal to cope with field-pieces of like calibre, which by their greater weight can use higher charges, and are therefore, far more powerful, particularly in developing the effects of shrapnel. This is obvious, if it be considered that a 12-pdr. gun will well bear four pound charges, while the howitzers are lively with one-fourth of the quantity of powder.

The absence of a limber and its caissons will also tend to impress a recollection of the auxiliary character of a naval force when landed; and, as before stated, if the operation be conducted within the legitimate sphere pertaining to it, this appendage will be found useless and cumbersome, and the want of it will answer as a proper check on any attempt to go beyond due limits, and thus expose the party to certain defeat or capture.

Should circumstances ever arise which would render the employment of seamen indispensable in the field, as in California, then the proper authorities will take care to provide for the occasion.

But in any case, it is not to be expected that seamen are to match good infantry; and to train them to perform more than the part of auxiliaries in military affairs, would be probably to sacrifice much of their usefulness in sailor-craft.

Since the introduction of the present system of howitzers for the armament of boats, in 1849, but little occasion has presented for their use, inasmuch as the United States has been in a state of peace with other nations. Still some cases have occurred in which it has been necessary to display force or to resort to it, and wherein the boat howitzers have taken a part. These are briefly stated in the following accounts taken from the official record and given in the order of their date.

U. S. FRIGATE CONSTITUTION—COM. MAYO.

September 14*th*, 1853.

A Report of Commodore Mayo, dated as above, from Emina, West Coast of Africa, gives the Navy Department the following account of a successful effort to terminate the hostilities existing between some of the native African tribes.

"On arriving at Cape Palmas, it was represented to me by Governor McGill, the chief Magistrate of the American Colony at this place, that a vexatious and somewhat sanguinary war had, for the last three years, existed between one of the Barbo tribes, on the left bank of the Cavalla river, and a Gribo tribe, upon the opposite bank. This war had interrupted the usual trade of the coast, had created alarm and distrust among the coasting vessels, and had in various ways proved injurious to the interests of American Colonists in that quarter.

Governor McGill in the most urgent terms solicited my interference to bring about a cessation of hostilities, and the chiefs of some of the native towns also sent me a petition to the same effect.

Moved by these applications and by my own desire to prevent unnecessary bloodshed, I proceeded in this ship to Cavalla river (about 15 miles from Cape Palmas,) on the 4th inst.—and immediately sent boats to communicate with the contending parties. The Gribo tribe gladly accepted my intervention, but the more warlike Barboes, rudely repelled my messenger, threatening to put him to death.

On the morning of the 5th, I left the ship with five armed boats, bearing a white flag, and went as near the beach as the heavy surf would permit. Again sending a messenger with a white flag (the head Krooman) I urged this fierce people to consent to an adjustment of this quarrel, but they again rudely repelled my messenger, and defied my power;

daring me to land, and using terms which, among themselves, are considered equivalent to a declaration of war. Finding it necessary to intimidate them, I threw a few light signal rockets over their town, to drive the women and children to the shelter of the neighboring forest, and then from the launch's gun threw a few shells over their houses. Being wholly unused to such projectiles, and very much alarmed by their explosion, they gladly hung out a white flag, and humbly expressed their willingness for peace.

On the following day it was again impossible for the boats to land, but I succeeded in getting a deputation on board the Constitution from each tribe, whereupon a "Grand Palaver" was held and peace agreed upon. On the morning of the 6th, other deputations came on board, the peace was ratified with all the formalities peculiar to the country, and I sailed for the Gulf of Guinea, most happy to have terminated this affair without bloodshed.

Lieut. Decamp who commanded the launch says,—"The sea broke with great violence on the coast, and it was impossible to effect a landing in the ship's boats." * * "I was ordered by the Commodore to open fire with the howitzer, (a 12-pdr. of 750 lbs.), but to fire high. Some thirty shrapnel were fired over the town, distant about six hundred yards, when a white flag was displayed from the beach. The firing ceased, &c. During our practice with the howitzer, five shot were fired per minute, and all but one exploded at the proper time and place; one lodged in the trunk of a cocoa-nut tree in the centre of the town, and the fuze failed to ignite the charge. The chief, 'Jim Peter,' sent word to know if we would extract it, or else inform him 'when it would burst.' * * Taking into consideration the roughness of the sea, our want of practice, &c., the affair was quite satisfactory to us. The gun threw with great precision and at a much greater range than I had any idea it would."

Lieut. Decamp recommends that the officer in charge should take great care to see that the compressors are screwed down when firing rapidly, and this becomes absolutely indispensable in a sea-way.

U. S. SHIP PLYMOUTH.

Shanghai, April 4th, 1854.

The lives and property of American and British citizens having been frequently endangered by the wanton proceedings of a body of Chinese Imperialists, encamped about Shanghai, which were persevered in, notwithstanding the representations of Captain Kelly, U. S. N., and Captain O'Callaghan, R. N., it was agreed by them to co-operate in abating the nuisance. To this effect, these officers, with the Consuls of their nations, made a formal request of the Chinese commander that he would cause the post to be peaceably evacuated, and notified him of their intention to enforce this request, if not otherwise complied with. No answer being received, there were landed, in the afternoon of the 4th of April, about 60 seamen and marines, with a 12-pdr. howitzer, in charge of Lieut. Guest, from the Plymouth, and 150 men from the British vessels "Encounter" and "Grecian."

These being joined by volunteers from the residents of Shanghai, with two private field-pieces, and 30 seamen from American merchant ships, the attack was commenced by Captain O'Callaghan, on the right of the entrenched camp, and by Captain Kelly on the left, who, about 4 P. M., directed a fire to be opened from the light artillery of his party.

Lieut. Guest, of the Plymouth, speaking of the U. S. 12-pdr. boat howitzer, which was under his charge, and had his personal direction, says:—

"Shell, shrapnel, and canister were fired, with great effect, perhaps to the number of 40 or 50 rounds."

"The fixed ammunition was perfect; not a single shell failed to burst, not a fuze or a tube disappointed us; and, consequently, the officers and men were inspired with perfect confidence in the gun, both as a means of assailing the enemy and of defence when attacked."

"The graduated fuzes so plainly marked from 1 to 5 seconds, enabled us to drop our shells exactly in the spot intended, and the precision with which it was done, in comparison with all other artillery which we had seen fired, was a subject of gratification and surprise.

"With the canister, we raked the top of the Chinese breastworks, and drove back a very large force, which advanced against us in the field. We found the gun as well adapted to canister as to shell or shrapnel."

Captain Kelly states, in his official Report, that after firing 15 or 20 minutes from the light artillery, the men were led forward, much exposed to the musketry and wall-pieces of the camp. Very soon the Chinese were routed, with some loss; and the next day the entrenchments were levelled, which terminated the annoyance.

The Americans and English had two seamen killed and six wounded. Mr. Gray, the chief clerk of a commercial house, lost both of his legs; and Captain Pearson (of an American merchant ship) was mortally wounded.

Expedition to Japan, 1853–54.

Commanded by Commodore M. C. Perry.

Though the peaceful tenor of the enterprise did not, most happily, in any case require a resort to arms, yet, as the people of the country were entirely strangers to the visitors, there was an imperative necessity for every precaution that could be used to guard against possible contingencies: as an omission to do so might not only have involved the lives of many officers and men, but have led to failure in accomplishing the main object of the mission itself.

The landing parties were therefore always well armed, and attended by some of the boat howitzers, with which the Squadron had been unusually well provided.* In some instances, the escort numbered 500 bayonets, and several howitzers on their field-carriages; a force much larger than the objects or means of our limited squadrons usually permit, and, under the circumstances, sufficiently strong to command respect, or to secure a way back to the boats.

In the course of this duty, the entire round of operations with Naval Light Artillery was often executed;—the preparation in boats,—the transferring of the pieces to their field-carriages,—the debarking and the march.

The landing of the howitzer, which, even when unopposed, as in this case, requires,

* One 24-pdr. and eleven 12-pdrs.

perhaps, more coolness and practice than any other of the manœuvres, is well illustrated by the sketch at the front of the volume, representing the debarkation of the escort to attend Commodore Perry, when going to meet the Imperial Commissioners of Japan. It is executed by Mr. Brown, one of the artists of the Expedition, who witnessed it from a convenient station opposite the spot, and furnishes a view of the principal incidents of the operation:—One howitzer mounted in the boat, another on its field-carriage in passing along the skids from the launch to the beach, —a third being dragged up the bank,—while a fourth is in readiness for the march.

One of these pieces was left in Japan, upon the departure of the Squadron, as it appears from the following communication to the Navy Department, published in the Congressional Document, No. 34, page 151.

Commodore Perry to the Secretary of the Navy.

U. S. Flag Ship Powhatan.

Off the town of Kanagawa,
Yedo Bay, Japan, April 4th, 1854.

Sir: The only favor asked by the Japanese commissioners has been that I would give to three of their number, each a brass howitzer and launch, equipped in the manner of those belonging to the squadron. This request was repeatedly made.

My reply was, that the boats and guns formed parts of the equipments of the ships, and could not be spared; but as the Saratoga was going home, I would venture to give them the gun belonging to her, and to recommend that the Government should send out to Japan, by some convenient opportunity, two more, &c., &c., &c.

U. S. STEAMER QUEEN,* LIEUT. COMMAND'G PREBLE.

Hong-Kong, Nov. 5th, 1855.

This offcer reports to Commander Joel Abbot, that the "Queen" left Hong-Kong at noon for Macao on the 2d of November. In passing the south side of Lantao Island, some fishing boats gave intelligence that they had been plundered by a number of piratical junks, which were then at anchor in the harbor of Tyloo, some five miles distant. The Queen steered in that direction, and ten junks were soon discovered at anchor with no colors flying: when within musket range of them, the engine was stopped, as the Queen (drawing seven feet) was then in eight feet water. Upon which the largest junk fired two shots at her in rapid succession, one of which struck the water close astern; this was returned by Lieut. Preble from the 12-pdr. boat-howitzer, which was the only gun that bore, and also

* A small steamer of about 150 tons, chartered by Commodore Perry to assist in protecting American citizens and their property near Canton. She was armed with four 4-pdrs. and a boat-gun transferred from one of the U. S. ships.

by a fire of musketry. All the junks now opened a fire of heavy guns, and the Queen, as soon as possible, brought her broadside guns (iron 4-pdrs.) to bear, firing round and grape. The largest junk, which was also the nearest, began to sweep towards the shore, but the others kept up a brisk and well-directed fire from their guns, the steamer being struck three times by shot, one of which proved to be a 6-pdr. Meanwhile, the 12-pdr. howitzer and broadside 4-pdrs. were actively employed, but the recoil of the latter was so severe that they nearly capsized when discharged, and one of them split a truck and axle, while another parted its breeching and split the coin.

The 12-pdr. howitzer, being mounted on a field-carriage, had to be lashed to the deck, and after the 6th round, bounded clear off the topgallant forecastle. However, several shells from it were seen to take effect on the junks, and Lieut. Preble learned afterwards from the Chinese that a number of the pirates were killed and wounded.

After firing ten shells from the howitzer, and 21 round shot and grape from the 4-pdrs.

with 200 rounds from the muskets, Lieut. Preble found the fire of the pirates so much superior to his own, that, being unable to board them from the steamer on account of the shallowness of the water, and having no suitable boat for the purpose, he hauled the "Queen" off, in order to go in quest of assistance. Arriving at Macao that evening, the intelligence was communicated to H. B. M. Steamer "Encounter," and next morning (the 3d) both vessels proceeded to the place, when the piratical junks were discovered at anchor in a small creek, to which they had moved in the absence of the "Queen." The "Encounter" had to anchor in four fathoms water, and Lieut. Preble says he then stood in again "to try the range of the howitzer on their new position. When in seven and a half feet water opened with it on them; they at once returned our fire, their shot passing beyond and close to us. We burst a 5 second shell directly in the town behind the junks, and sent a 4 second shell which burst directly over them. We tried two more shells which scattered a little short of them. At the fourth discharge, our howitzer having been completely disabled by the breaking of a wheel of the carriage, I backed out, and returned towards the "Encounter."*

The two vessels being reinforced by the British Steamer "Baracouta," with boats and men from H. B. M. ships "Winchester" and "Spartan," the "Encounter" opened her 10-in. guns on the pirates, the shells falling with precision into the town, which was speedily deserted. The boats now landed and burned 17 junks, after removing the most of their guns to the British vessels; some of them were 24-pdrs. After which the "Queen" left, and proceeded to Hong Kong.

In conclusion, Lieut. Preble suggests a heavier and better mounted battery for the "Queen" and asks that "a gun slide for the howitzer" may be made without delay on board the Macedonian from the pattern there.

---

* Firing from the howitzer on its field carriage aboard ship, should never be practised, as this carriage is only intended for operations on land.

U. S. Steamer Powhatan, Capt. McCluney. Chinese Seas.

Under date of August 8th, 1855, the Commander of this vessel, then at Hong-Kong, informs the Navy Department of an attack upon a large fleet of piratical junks by the boats of the Powhatan and H. B. M. Steam Sloop Rattler, under the direction of Captain Fellowes of the latter.

It appears that on the 2d of August, Captain Fellowes returned from a cruize, and informed Captain McCluney that he had chased a large fleet of piratical junks into the small harbor of Koolan, about 60 miles from Hong-Kong, but the water being too shallow to admit of the Rattler pursuing them, and not having a sufficient number of boats to attack so large a force, Captain Fellowes returned to Hong-Kong to ask the co-operation and assistance of Captain McCluney which was most cheerfully rendered, in the manner detailed in the following report of Lieut. Pegram, who commanded the division of boats from the Powhatan.

U. S. STEAM FRIGATE POWHATAN.
Hong-Kong, *August* 6*th*, 1855.

SIR :—

I have to report that the Boat expedition which left this ship on the 3d instant, consisting of the 1st and 2d Launches and 1st cutter, each mounting a 12-pdr. howitzer and carrying in all 100 men (placed under command of Commander William A. Fellowes of H. B. M. steam-sloop Rattler, for the purpose of attacking a large fleet of piratical junks, which has recently been committing extensive depredations on commerce in these seas) was taken in tow by the "Rattler" the same day, and conveyed to Koolan Island, her draught not allowing her to proceed further.

On the 4th, shortly after daylight, the boats were taken in tow by the "Eaglet" (steam-tender). Passing Koolan Bay, no indications of pirates being found, stood over to the northward and eastward.

At 7 A. M., discovered a lorcha endeavoring to escape, which induced Captain Fellowes to dispatch the "Rattler's" pinnace and the Powhatan's 1st cutter in pursuit. After an energetic chase of about two hours she was brought to by the firing from the Rattler and the boats, when she hoisted English colors. On being boarded, her master, who was an European, produced his papers, which were found to be correct. He declared he had been in the hands of the pirates the night before, who had robbed his vessel of every thing of value. She was then ordered to anchor under the guns of the Rattler.

About the time the boats got alongside the lorcha, we discovered a large junk standing out of a narrow passage, which on seeing us put back. We gave chase and shortly came in sight of a large fleet of heavy war junks at anchor with their flags and streamers flying, evidently well prepared for our reception. Before getting in range, they opened fire which was returned by the "Eaglet" from a 24 lb. rocket tube, with such startling effect that the whole fleet were soon seen hoisting sail. The Powhatan's two launches, and three boats belonging to the Rattler (with musketeers on board) now started in chase.

On coming within howitzer range we commenced a brisk fire of shrapnel, when the two largest junks rounded to and fired a heavy broadside, the round shot passing over the boats and the grape splashing the water in every direction, but without other effect than to cause the men to spring to the oars with more life and energy to get within canister range.

From rapid firing, the guns were much heated, and we had use for all our remaining shrapnel. In this manner a brisk fire was kept up, until within a hundred yards, when canister and musketry soon decided the contest.

Lieut. Rolando, who was the first to reach the nearest and heaviest junk, (carrying upwards of 20 guns) with a cheer boarded her, took possession and hoisted our colors. I immediately stood for another junk, which had the chief's flag flying, and getting a raking position poured in a destructive fire of canister, which soon cleared her decks, when we boarded and hoisted our flag. Captain Fellowes, who was on board almost simultaneously with ourselves, hauled down the pirate's flag, to which, being in command of the expedition, he was of course entitled. This junk mounted above 20 pieces of heavy calibre, none less than 18-pdrs. I left our acting boatswain, Mr. Bailey, in charge of her, and lost no time in pursuing the other junks, which were now endeavoring to make their escape with oars and sails.

From this time, the boats for the most part acted singly in the work of destruction, and it is therefore impossible to give more than a partial account of the different actions of the day.

The coolness and gallantry of our leader, (Captain Fellowes) elicited the admiration of all. With his gig's crew and five musketeers he had engaged a large war junk, when Lieut. Rolando coming up to his assistance, took her by boarding, after encountering a hand-to-hand resistance amid a shower of spears and combustible missiles. I regret to state that, after being boarded she was blown up by one of the pirate's crew, who fighting courageously was forced below, and is supposed in his desperation to have fired a train communicating with the magazine. The effects were most disastrous, capsizing the Rattler's gig, blowing Captain Fellowes overboard, together with Lieut. Rolando and a number of the Powhatan's men, killing two and severely wounding others, one of whom has since died. I further regret to report, that but a moment prior to this, Private Adamson of the marines (whose courage and daring in several previous encounters during the day, had attracted my notice) was shot severely in the groin, after being one of the first to gain the enemy's deck.

Paymaster Brownson, in charge of one of the Rattler's boats, under the most trying circumstances, during which three of his men lost their lives, and his boat enveloped in smoke and flame, evinced a courage and presence of mind, rarely to be surpassed. Mr. James, Boatswain of the same ship, after a severe encounter with a heavy junk, succeeded in boarding her in a gallant manner.

The Rattler's pinnace with Lieuts. Wrex, Green, and Lomax, and the Powhatan's cutter with Master E. T. McCauley in charge, accompanied by Assistant Engineer Kellogg, were so far away from the scene of action, in pursuit of the lorcha before mentioned, that it was impossible for them to participate in the more exciting events of the day, notwithstanding they made every exertion to do so. They arrived, however, in time to render very essential service in taking off the prize crews and burning and blowing up the captured junks, which, the shoalness of the water, prevented the steamer from towing off.

Lieut. Jones, in command of the marines, was unfortunately so ill as to be prohibited by the medical officers from joining in the action; yet so great was his anxiety to engage, that I had to interpose my authority in the most positive manner to prevent his doing so.

During the action, ten war junks mounting on an average 16 or 18 guns, from 6-pdrs. to 68-pdrs. were burned, blowed up and destroyed. Six captured junks' lorchas were recaptured, one of which being aground was burned, the others replaced under convoy of the Eaglet. Sixteen smaller junks made their escape.

It is impossible to state the exact number of pirates killed, wounded, and drowned, during the engagement, but it is estimated between 500 and 600, as the decks were covered with the bodies of the slain, and the water with drowning men. The pirates numbered about 1500 men.

It would be invidious to attempt a comparison between the officers and men of the two services engaged. Their union on the occasion served to heighten the enthusiasm of both to such a degree as to ensure success.

I refer you to the enclosed Report of Assistant Surgeon Albert Schriver, for an account of the casualties of the day. His prompt and untiring efforts, in connection with those of Surgeon Pritchard and Assistant Surgeon Wilson of the Rattler, in relation to the sufferings of the wounded, are worthy of the highest praise.

In connection with this report, I deem it not inappropriate to express my great satisfaction at the performance of the 12-pdr. boat howitzer of Lieut. Dahlgren's construction. For rapidity and precision of fire, facility of working, certainty of execution, and completeness of arrangement of ammunition, I have never seen any thing to compare with them.

I am, sir, very respectfully,
Your obed't serv't,

[Signed] R. B. PEGRAM,
Senior Lieut. in charge of the Powhatan's Boat Expedition.

To
CAPTAIN WM. J. MCCLUNEY,
Commanding U. S. ship Powhatan.

P. S. I omitted in the body of this Report to mention that Acting Master's Mate Samuel R. Craig, accompanied Lieut. Rolando in the 2d launch, and rendered material assistance during the day.

POWHATAN.

Killed—Two seamen.

Mortally wounded—One seaman and one marine.

Wounded—Two lieutenants and 8 seamen

Total, 14 American.

RATTLER.

Killed—One gunner, Royal Marine Artillery, and two seamen and one marine.

Wounded—Three gunners, Royal Marine Artillery, 3 seamen and one boy.

Total, 11 English.

Making a general total of 25 American and English killed and wounded.

APPENDIX.

As a knowledge of the means employed by others may be considered next in importance to a knowledge of our own means, the following account of the Boat Armament of a principal maritime power is appended to this memorandum.

It has the advantage of official authority, being extracted from the "Aide Mémoire Navale," issued in 1850, by the sanction of the Minister of Marine.

BOAT ARMAMENT OF THE FRENCH NAVY.

UNTIL recently, the French system of armament for boats was as follows:—

	18-pdr. Carronades.	12-pdr. Carronades.	Swivels.	Blunder-busses	Mountain Howitzers.
Ships of 82 and razees	1	1	4	8	2
24-pdr. Frigates		2	4	8	2
18-pdr. Frigates and razees of 28		1	4	8	2
Corvettes and brigs of 18 and 16		1	4	6	1
Gun brigs			4	4	
Transports over 380 tons			4	6	
	lbs.	lbs.	lbs.	lbs.	lbs.
Weight	1274	840	187	44	220
Charge	2.2	1.43	.29	.11	.6

It is stated (Colonel Charpentier) that the mountain howitzer was introduced into the French naval service by the Prince de Joinville; during the expedition under Admiral Baudin to Vera Cruz, he had the opportunity of experiencing how useful even so trifling a piece may be.

The present system of boat armament as re-organized by a general order of 27th November, 1849, is thus·

	Number of Boats.	Bronze Howitzers* and Boat-Carriages.			Field Carriages for Mountain 12.
		15-cent.	New 12-cent.	Mountain 12.	
LINE-OF-BATTLE SHIPS.					
Launch . . .	1	1			
1st cutter . .	1	1			
Barge	1			1	
2d cutter . .	1			1	1
Other cutters . .	2			1	
1ST CLASS FRIGATES.					
Launch . . .	1	1			
1st cutter . .	1	1			
Barge	1			1	
2d cutter . .	1			1	1
Other cutters . .	1			1	1
2D AND 3D CLASS FRIGATES.					
Launch . . .	1	1			
1st cutter . .	1		1		
Barge	1			1	
2d cutter . .	1			1	1
Other cutters . .	1			1	1
1ST AND 2D CLASS CORVETTES.					
Launch . . .	1		1		
1st cutter . .	1			1	1
Barge	1				
2d cutter . .	1				
Other cutters . .	1				
3D CLASS CORVETTES.					
Launch . . .	1		1		
1st cutter . .	1			1	1
2d cutter . . .	1				
1ST AND 2D CLASS BRIGS.					
Launch . . .	1		1		
1st cutter . .	1			1	1
2d cutter . . .	1				

* The 15-cent. may be considered as equivalent to our 24-pdr.; the 12-cent to our 12-pdr.

Hence it appears that carronades, swivels, and blunderbusses have been laid aside, and an entire system of howitzers substituted. A desire having been manifested by some officers of rank to include the field howitzer of 16-cent., a special commission was ordered to consider the proposition; the report was unanimously against the piece, as too heavy for boats.

The new howitzer of 12-cent. or 12-pdr., created particularly for boat service, is a necessary intermediate between the 15-cent. or 24-pdr. of 581^{k} and the mountain 12 of 220lbs.

It will be perceived that the mountain 12 is the only piece intended to be landed, and to this end it has the same field-carriage as that used in the army. The "Aide Mémoire Navale" (568) remarks, in connection with this subject:—

"If the bronze howitzer of 15-cent. be definitely adopted (which has since been done by the order of November, 1849,) it will probably be inconvenient to put on board its field-carriage, as proposed in 1842 by the *Conseil de travaux*. It would be too cumbersome in the ship, and would be of no great service in landing by reason of the difficulty of drawing it by hand, and of disembarking it. The mountain carriage in use is fully sufficient. It has the advantage, from its ease of movement and manœuvre, of being able to penetrate sufficiently into the interior of a country."

The system of boat armament in the two navies may be compared thus:

		24-pdr.	Medium 12-pdr.	Light 12-pdr.
		Inches.	Inches.	Inches.
U. S. Navy	Diameter bore	5.82	4.62	4.62
	Weight lbs.	1300	760	430
		Inches.	Inches.	Inches.
French Navy	Diam. bore	5.96	4.75	4.75
	Weight lbs.	1280	660	220

The French calibres are greater than the American by a very trifling quantity. Their weight of piece rather inferior, considerably so in the medium 12-pdr., and much more so in the light 12-pdr.

In landing for field operations, there is only the 3d class piece provided on one side, and on the other the pieces of the 2d and 3d class, though the latter are not so numerous.

Two ammunition boxes are allowed to the Mountain 12 on shore, containing each seven shells and one stand of canister.

RIFLED ARMS.

RIFLED MUSKETS.

THIS memorandum was intended to treat exclusively of the Armament of Boats with light artillery. There is another weapon, however, of recent date, which should not be passed by without notice here, because it is an important adjunct to the howitzer or to any other kind of light gun whether used in boats or elsewhere, and is asserted by some to be even capable of overmatching artillery, as it certainly is all other kinds of musketry. I speak of the rifled musket, whether in the Delvigne, the Minie, or the English form.

The Delvigne, which has the priority in point of date over the other two, is rifled and has an upright pin (tige*) screwed into or forming part of the breech plug.

The shot is conical and descends freely into the barrel, until its base rests on the head of the pin. (Plate 12, No. 2.)

---

* Hence called the "carabine à tige," sketched in plate 12.

The ramrod (hollowed at the end to the conical form of the shot,) is now applied, and with a few blows forces the base of the shot to expand, so that it can no longer issue from the piece without following the direction given by the rifle grooves,—hence the rotatory movement.

Major Minie obtains a like result by the shot alone, which is made of a conical form, and has a cavity at the base, into which is inserted a cup or plug of harder metal than the lead. The shot is fired from any piece made and rifled in the ordinary manner. (Plate 12, No. 5.)

The force of the charge operating on the cup or plug, forces it into the cavity at the base of the shot, expands it, and thus compels it to follow the course of the grooving in the barrel.

By the English method, the conical shot is merely hollowed at the base, and is expanded by the entrance of the gas from the charge into the cavity,—so that both the Delvigne and Minie expedients for forcing or slugging the shot are dispensed with. (Plate 12, No. 4.)

All of these contrivances appear to answer

the end proposed; that is, the greater weight of the projectile and the decreased relative resistance it experiences by preserving the apex in front, give great superiority of range and accuracy to the conical shot.

Which of them combines the most advantages in the mode of application, remains to be seen. The Delvigne shot is more simple than that of Minie; but the piece less so; whilst the English system is perfectly simple in the musket and its shot, and in this respect, has the advantage over both of the French arrangements.

Whether the principle by which it is forced, is so good as that of Delvigne or of Minie, and will give as accurate results, we are without other data to judge by than those which have guided the choice of the parties concerned.

It is certain that the British musket must have inferior penetrating power to either of the French pieces,—in proportion to the weights of ball.

To this it may be answered, that the power of the English shot is quite sufficient for its purpose, and being lighter than that of the

French, a greater number of rounds can be carried,—while the musket being also lighter, relieves the soldier of so much additional weight.

As regards the weight of shot, it may be that the English is all sufficient, and therefore the French more heavy than is necessary; but in the absence of the experience which battles and campaigns alone can furnish, it must be remembered that the efficiency of musketry depends mainly on the weight of the ball, and that it may be a perilous experiment to err against this axiom.

Leaving the question, however, so far as it concerns the land service, to be settled by those whose province it is, and whose experience best fits them to resolve the problem, it is certainly most advisable that the naval musket should not sacrifice the undenied advantage of calibre for any other attributed to a lighter ball or a lighter musket.

Because its use is restricted almost entirely to the ship or the boat, where we know the weight of the common musket is perfectly manageable by any man of ordinary strength, and is also that which, for a long time, has had the sanction of experience in all armies. The seaman too has but to bear the weight of ammunition where he stands, and finds the additional supply almost at his elbow. If he lands, which, as already observed, is seldom and cannot be assumed to be among the professed and legitimate purposes of his vocation, his marches are short; he does not travel day after day like an infantry man, lugging along his musket and its ammunition, together with a knapsack and other miscellaneous incumbrances; sometimes performing forced marches under this burden. On the contrary, he rarely goes far from the landing or remains long.

No one of the conditions then, that have induced the reduction of calibre for the land forces, can apply to the marine musket. Wherefore, it would be unwise for the navy to assume voluntarily and without occasion, a disadvantage which necessity may impose on the other service.

If the heavier shot has more force than is required for its sure effect upon personal, fairly exposed to view, it is to be borne in mind, that the circumstances where it will be used afloat, frequently interpose many obstacles which may lessen that effect, so far as to entirely nullify the lighter shot.

While discussing the subject in England, the well-known persistency of the Duke of Wellington in opposing any reduction of calibre, notwithstanding the gain that might accrue to the movement of the soldier or to the repetition of his fire, was often cited: and it cannot be denied that the opinions of so able and experienced a commander, should out-weigh all nice differences. The "feu meurtriere" of the British musket has been admitted by one of the ablest writers of the day, who spoke from experience as well as from mature reflection on the subject. (Jomini.)

Its calibre was 0.702 in., while the French musket had a calibre of 0.689 in., and the disadvantage of this apparently slight difference, seems to have been appreciated by the French authorities. For according to Colonel Charpentier,* it so manifestly subjected their line

* Page 431.

to a certain inferiority when compared with the musketry of other European nations, that in 1842, the Minister of War decided upon 18 $^{mm.}$, (0.709 in.,) as the calibre of the musket, the charge being 123 grains (8 grammes.)

The light shot may be as fatal as the heavier, but the effect of its shock on many parts of the human frame is not equally capable of disabling an adversary, however deadly to him it may prove eventually.

Conical shot have perhaps proportionally less power of shock than round balls, and are more liable to be diverted from their course when they come in contact with a resisting surface which is oblique to their direction. Besides their form is calculated to pierce the substances through which they pass with far less detriment to the texture; so that the wound is remediable, when that of a round ball of like weight, would have been beyond the reach of surgical skill.

Thus in many personal encounters, it may be observed that one party has a revolver, the other a bowie-knife; the latter receives several shots in approaching which may cause his death afterwards, but from deficient power of shock are not disabling at the time, and he succeeds in fatally hurting his antagonist.

The small pointed shot of the common revolver has even been known to pierce vital parts with little permanent injury. In one of recent occurrence, the shot entered at the back, passed through the lungs and was cut out of the breast; the wounded man recovered in three weeks. Another received the shot through the liver and kidneys, but got well after an illness of some months.

I do not mean to assert that the English conical shot or the French is, the former so light, or the latter so acute, that either would have been likely to make wounds of so little consequence; but it is not less probable that the powers of both might be improved by a different combination of weight and form, and thus be rendered effective under circumstances requiring the utmost development of power.

For these reasons it is conceived that the following general conditions are entitled to consideration in selecting a rifled musket for the navy.

1st. The piece should not be lighter than

the present musket in common use for the army and navy, nor its calibre materially less.

2nd. This weight of arm and diameter of bore will admit of the greatest weight of ball that has been used. The present French Regulation shot weighs 733 grains,—the charge 69½ grains. The English shot weighs about 520 grains,* and the charge of a cartridge, carefully weighed, gave 73½ grains, though this seems to be larger than that mentioned by some writers—(2¼ drs.)

I have witnessed practice with shot of 834 grains (nearly 2 ounces) fired from an ordinary musket (charge 73 grains) rifled for the purpose. The practice was sustained for half an hour, the shot falling some 1300 yards distant and very closely; the reaction of the musket did not appear to inconvenience the marksman.

3rd. The shot should not be very acute in front, as such form is more liable to have its apex displaced from the axis of the bore, and hence increased inaccuracy of flight,—but it

* Sketched in plate 12.

should be cylindric at the base and terminating with a conical front which ought rather to be rounded like the English than acute like the French. The latter presents less resistance to the air and to substances which it may enter, but of these abundant properties it may well spare something in order to gain more power of shock, &c., &c.

4th. The barrel should be shorter, however, than that of the U. S. smooth bored musket, as all length that is not indispensable to accuracy is inconvenient for boat service. The French Delvigne musket has a bore about 33½ inches long, which is nearly 8 inches shorter than our service musket.*

5th. With a like weight and length the barrel may be better fortified with metal about the location of the charge, than that of the common musket, and the alleged superiority of decarbonized steel for gun barrels, should be considered.

---

* Colonel Gordon (p. 42) says the length of barrel should not be less than 30 to 32 inches,—and that the best shooting at Enfield, during the trials of various pieces, was made with the artillery carbine which had a barrel 30 inches long.

6th. The present bayonet, which is the most useless thing in the world except at the end of the musket, may be replaced by another, fashioned like a stout sword or bowie-knife, which will be quite as serviceable for its peculiar purpose and useful in many others besides.

The manner of expanding or forcing the ball, the number of grooves, depth, twist and other details, can only be determined by experiment, as well as the actual development of the general principles which have been noted above to be most conducive to the power of the arm.

Until a proper arm can be provided, a substitute may be had by rifling the present musket; and this is contemplated by the Bureau,—but such an arrangement should be in force no longer than is required to decide on and obtain the proper arm.

Many varieties of rifled muskets have been devised and tried,—the following account of some of them is extracted from the Essay of Colonel Gordon:—

RIFLED MUSKETS.

		Regulations Minie, 1851.	New Enfield, 1853.	U. S. Percussion Musket.	Wilkinson.	Lancaster.	Purdy.		Lovell.	The Brunswick.
Barrel-weight . . .	oz.	74	66	68	65	78	63¼		65½	62
Barrel-length . .	in.	39	39	42	39	39	39		39	30
Bore diam.	in.	.702	.577	.69	.530	.550 / .540	.650		.635	.704
Grooves	No / one turn	4 / 78	3 / 78	Smooth.	5 / 78	Eliptic'l Smooth	4 / 64 Increase.		4 / 78	2 / 30
Charge . , . . .	grs.	68	62*	100	68	68	68		68	68
Bullet		Minie.	Solid Exp'd	Round.	Solid Exp'd	Plug. Exp'd	Minie. Heavy	Minie. Light	Minie.	Round Belted.
Bullet diam. . . .	in.	.690	.568	.65	.537	.532	.630	.628	.630	.696
Bullet length . .	in.	1.030	.960		1.075	1.125	1.145	.948	1.145	
Bullet weight . . .	grs.	680	520	412	500	542	.686	.562	686	557
Musket and Bayonet	lbs.	10.55	9.19	9.82	9.31	9.56	9.1		9.10	11.35
60 rounds . . .	lbs.	6.76	5.23		4.98					5.60
P. B. (feet 4.65) . .	Yards.	177			185	194	190	176	176	173
Elevation. For 100	"	0° 14′			0° 14′	0° 11′	11′	14′	0° 11′	0° 08′
" 200	"	0° 39′			0° 28′	0° 26′	26′	26′	0° 26′	0° 34′
" 300	"	0° 53′			0° 47′	0° 49′	49′	52′	0° 49′	0° 54′
" 400	"	1° 22′			1° 05′	1° 09′	1° 9′	1° 18′	1° 09′	1° 26′
" 500	"	1° 51′			1° 25′	1° 34′	1° 34′	1° 47′	1° 34′	Too wild
" 600	"	2° 23′			2°	2° 02′	2° 2′	Too wild to give a correct angle.	2° 02′	
" 700	"	3° 05′			2° 29′	2° 32′	2° 32′		2° 32′	
" 800	"	3° 25′			2° 44′	3° 01′	2° 50′		2° 50′	
" 900	"									
" 1000	"				4° 31′				4° 16′	

* Gordon 43. A cartridge said to have been obtained from an authentic source contained 73 grains.

In connection with these general remarks upon rifled muskets, a few words may not be inappropriate upon another mode of rifling the ball, and the style of arm selected for the purpose.

Great ingenuity has in late years been exercised upon breech-loading arms in this country. Hall, Cochrane, Colt, Sharp, Perry, Jennings, Marston, Greene and many others, have contributed most successfully to the solution of this problem, though in view of the amazing variety of their devices, the combinations and the mechanical skill exhibited, it may perhaps be doubted whether they have yet exhausted this interesting and fertile subject.

Many of these gentlemen are quite as skilful in the use, as in the design and execution of their weapons, which I have several times witnessed.

The performance of the Sharp and Perry rifles and carbines, are well known in the navy. The facility with which they are handled on the practice ground, the power and accuracy of their fire, are admirable. The chief difficulty would be to procure men, who would use without abusing these means, and to preserve the mechanism in good condition; not so much against the casualties of service as the neglect or ill-advised attentions of the store room, so fatal to many of the modern appliances that are consigned to its keeping.

It can hardly be said that any important advantage to accuracy or power can be derivable from loading at the breech, rather than at the muzzle. For there can be no weapon superior in either of these qualities to the American rifle, which belongs to the latter class.

The facility and convenience of loading, alone remains as the unquestioned peculiar property of charging at the breech.

In many cases this may be desirable, but as a general rule, masses of men can load and fire with the ordinary muzzle-loading muskets so much more rapidly than is consistent with good aim, as to render the practice a notorious and crying evil, which is frequently commented on by the best military writers. Take the following remarks from the Text Book of a French Military School.

"Let it be admitted that a battalion formed in double column, and distant rather more than 400 yards, is advancing upon another battalion in line of 256 files, firing from two ranks at the rate of 3 rounds a minute; if the attacking column steps $25\frac{1}{2}$ inches, and at the rate of 120 per minute, it would close with the enemy in five minutes: wherefore, in so doing, it would receive (512 × 15) 7,680 musket shots, but as the average number of hits from 400 yards to collision is about 50 per cent., the column would receive 3,840 bullets, and would be destroyed before reaching the line. No account is made of the two other battalions, which ought, however, to be very effective."

"With the flint muskets, and men not well practised, the average of hits would be reduced to one-third, and still 2,560 bullets would attain the column."

"But experience in the wars of the Empire proves that not even one-tenth of the effect just indicated can be relied on; it must therefore be admitted that the excitement of the conflict, the noise, the smoke, the dust, the rash haste of some, the dullness of others, prevent the soldier from aiming and making the best use of his weapon. The most perfect rifles cannot remedy this state of things. Our best disciplined troops never were able to control this kind of impulse and excitement, to which the French army owes the brightest page of its history."

"In the combats of lines of skirmishers, the same results are noticed, and the soldier fires almost mechanically before him; it is only when he is sheltered that he can give full effect to the accuracy of the arm."

Again, page 382:—"In general the infantry soldier, when excited by the combat, is far from making good use of the accuracy of his musket, which induces some officers to think that the most perfect arms would be of no great use to him. At a period when our troops were well inured to war, General Gassendi (of artillery) calculated that 3000 cartridges were expended for every man disabled. It is generally admitted that in the latter wars of the Empire, 10,000 cartridges were expended for every man that was killed."

Hence it is probable that the rifled musket which can be loaded about as readily as the smooth bored musket, furnishes all the facilities that are desirable for the ordinary purposes of an army.

It is not proper, however, to close the road to a full trial of this issue; the expenses incurred by the inventors, their great ability, and the excellence of their results, entitle the question to a full and impartial trial: which can readily be done by furnishing a number of the best kinds of breech-loading weapons to the different ships of the navy, so that at least one division of small-arm men may be so provided. Experience will, in time, supply the full amount of facts required to decide whether the muzzle-loading, or the breech-loading piece is to be preferred, in part or altogether; and how they shall be distributed so as to obtain the full advantage of either or both.

Among the advantages which have been attributed to the great range and force of the rifled musket, is its superiority to artillery, which, in the estimation of many, is thus to be deprived of its chief virtue and reduced to a very subordinate part. This, however, is not the opinion of two very eminent military writers, one English, the other French.

(Sir Howard Douglas, 531.) "Whilst we fully admit the vast importance of the rifle musket as a special arm, we must be permitted to doubt the correctness of the opinion that it will prevent artillery from keeping the field. Shrapnel shells will, undoubtedly, still prove an overpowering antagonist of infantry acting in swarms, *en tirailleur*, in the manner in which it is proposed to employ infantry armed with long range rifle-muskets."

"Under the powerful effect of shrapnel-shells, together with the menaces and charges of cavalry, clouds of infantry acting *en tirailleur*, will either be compelled to rally into masses, or to retire upon their supporting bodies, columns, or lines, when round shot will exercise its wonted power, and thus the battle will become general in the ordinary way."

"Should artillery be attacked by the enemy's riflemen, it should have recourse to spherical case shot; but if the circumstances of the case should be such that spherical case shot, improved as it now is, does not accomplish the end, then bodies of riflemen should be employed to do for the artillery what the latter cannot do for itself—repel those of the enemy."

(Thiroux, 135.) "It would seem that the perfecting of the infantry musket might lead to the disuse of artillery; but this is not at all so; on the contrary, we think that the value of this arm will be increased, inasmuch as the defence being rendered more energetic, obstacles, such as dwellings, farms, &c., which picked corps formerly carried by a vigorous and rapid assault, cannot now be taken without being first battered and fired by artillery, &c., &c., &c."

In the operations of the Crimea, where the armies of all the belligerents are equipped with the rifled musket of one kind or another, it does not seem that artillery is less resorted to than formerly, nor with less effect. In the heavy batteries where much annoyance had been experienced from the sharp-shooters, both parties found a remedy in the same weapon, and series of rifle pits were established for marksmen, on more extensive scales than formerly. These then became objects of interest, and their possession was fiercely contested hand to hand.

History does not record any instances where the fire of light and heavy ordnance was more murderous than at the Alma, Inkermann, Balaclava, Traktir, and in various phases of the siege. In the very last of the struggle at the Malakoff, we find the French wheeling up field guns to decide the result more promptly and effectively.

There is no doubt that each arm will have, as it always has had, its distinctive advantage and corresponding application.

In general the common opinion is liable to be violently impelled by first impressions, and is prone to exaggerate the powers of a new weapon; imagining that it will be likely to supplant all others. Subsequent experience as surely rectifies errors of this kind, and assigns to each its true value.

PLATE 12

ELONGATED SHOT.

full scale

3

AMERICAN
RIFLE

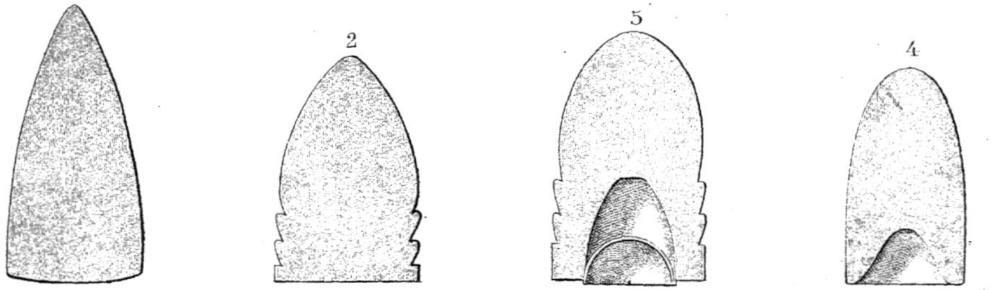

2

FRENCH
CARAB. À TIGE
(Delvigne)

5

MINIE
COMMON U.S. MUSKET
RIFLED

4

FOR NEW
BRIT MUSKET

1

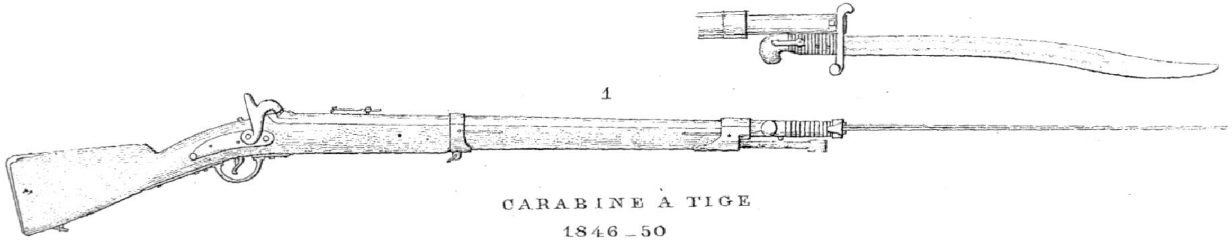

CARABINE À TIGE
1846_50

D. Chillas Lith. 50 S. 3 St. Phil.

EXPLANATION OF PLATE 12.

No. 1. Represents a "Carabine à tige" obtained from France. It bears the government inspection marks, and some of its details are recorded at page 193.

No. 2. The shot of this piece, weighing 733 grains.

No. 3. An American rifle shot, such as used during many years in the United States for fine target shooting. It weighs 732 grains,—is perfectly smooth and swaged to the most exact figure.

No. 4. A shot known as the Pritchett, for British regulation rifled musket; from a cartridge said to have been received from an authentic source.

No. 5. Is a Minie shot adopted to the common smooth bore when rifled. It weighs 834 grains.

ERRATA.

Page 105, first line of Note, for "Captain de Brette's," read Captain de Brettes.

Page 122, Note, sixth line from bottom, for "fixed a primer," read "fired" a primer.

Page 177, Second line from bottom, for "Lieut. Wrex," read "Lieut. Wrey."

Page 168, for "Commander," read "Commodore" Joel Abbot.

Page 204, in heading of table, for "Regulations," read "Regulation" Minié.

www.ingramcontent.com/pod-product-compliance
Lightning Source LLC
LaVergne TN
LVHW050525100826
845148LV00002B/442